WALKING IN
THE ISLES OF SCILLY

About the Author

Paddy Dillon is a prolific walker and guidebook writer, with over 60 books to his name and contributions to 30 other books. He has written for several outdoor magazines and other publications, and has appeared on radio and television.

Paddy uses a tablet computer to write as he walks. His descriptions are therefore precise, having been written at the very point at which the reader uses them.

He is an indefatigable long-distance walker who has walked all of Britain's National Trails and several European trails. He has also walked in Nepal, Tibet, Korea and the Rocky Mountains of Canada and the US. Paddy is a member of the Outdoor Writers and Photographers Guild.

Other Cicerone guides by the author

Glyndŵr's Way
Irish Coastal Walks
The Cleveland Way and the
    Yorkshire Wolds Way
The GR20 Corsica
The GR5 Trail
The Great Glen Way
The Irish Coast to Coast Walk
The Mountains of Ireland
The National Trails
The North York Moors
The Pennine Way
The Reivers Way
The South West Coast Path
The Teesdale Way
Trekking in Greenland
Trekking in the Alps (contributor)
Trekking through Mallorca

Walking and Trekking in Iceland
Walking in County Durham
Walking in Madeira
Walking in Mallorca
Walking in Malta
Walking in Menorca
Walking in Sardinia
Walking in the North Pennines
Walking on Gran Canaria
Walking on Guernsey
Walking on Jersey
Walking on La Gomera and
    El Hierro
Walking on La Palma
Walking on Tenerife
Walking on the Isle of Arran
Walking the Galloway Hills

WALKING IN
THE ISLES OF SCILLY

by
Paddy Dillon

2 POLICE SQUARE, MILNTHORPE, CUMBRIA LA7 7PY
www.cicerone.co.uk

© Paddy Dillon 2000, 2006, 2009, 2015

Fourth edition 2015
ISBN 978 1 85284 806 4

Third edition 2009
ISBN 978 1 85284 586 5
Second edition 2006
ISBN-10 1 85284 475 2
ISBN-13 978 1 85284 475 2
First edition 2000
ISBN 1 85284 310 1

Printed in China on behalf of Latitude Press Ltd
A catalogue record for this book is available from the British Library.
All photographs are by the author unless otherwise stated.

o⑤s Ordnance Survey® This product includes mapping data licensed from Ordnance Survey® with the permission of the Controller of Her Majesty's Stationery Office. © Crown copyright 2015. All rights reserved. Licence number PU100012932

The map on page 83 is used with permission of the Abbey Garden.

Updates to this Guide

While every effort is made by our authors to ensure the accuracy of guidebooks as they go to print, changes can occur during the lifetime of an edition. Any updates that we know of for this guide will be on the Cicerone website (www.cicerone.co.uk/806/updates), so please check before planning your trip. We also advise that you check information about such things as transport, accommodation and shops locally. Even rights of way can be altered over time. We are always grateful for information about any discrepancies between a guidebook and the facts on the ground, sent by email to info@cicerone.co.uk or by post to Cicerone, 2 Police Square, Milnthorpe LA7 7PY, United Kingdom.

Front cover: Looking from St Agnes to Gugh as the sea recedes from The Bar

CONTENTS

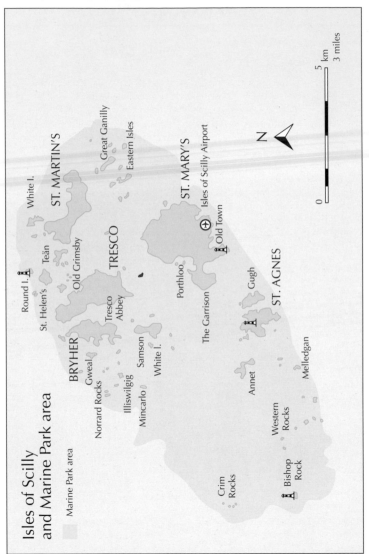

Isles of Scilly
and Marine Park area

Marine Park area

Crim Rocks
Bishop Rock
Western Rocks
Annet
Melledgan
Norrard Rocks
Gweal
BRYHER
Illiswilgig
Mincarlo
Samson
White I.
St. Helen's
Teän
Round I.
Old Grimsby
TRESCO
Tresco Abbey
ST. MARTIN'S
White I.
Great Ganilly
Eastern Isles
Porthloo
The Garrison
ST. MARY'S
Isles of Scilly Airport
Old Town
Gugh
ST. AGNES

N

0   km 5
    3 miles

INTRODUCTION

'Somewhere among the note-books of Gideon I once found a list of diseases as yet unclassified by medical science, and among these there occurred the word Islomania, which was described as a rare but by no means unknown affliction of spirit. There are people, Gideon used to say, by way of explanation, who find islands somehow irresistible. The mere knowledge that they are on an island, a little world surrounded by the sea, fills them with an indescribable intoxication.'

Lawrence Durrell, *Reflections on a Marine Venus*

Of all the British Isles, the Isles of Scilly are the most blessed. Basking in sunshine, rising green and pleasant from the blue Atlantic Ocean, fringed by rugged cliffs and sandy beaches, these self-contained little worlds are a joy to explore. They are as close to a tropical paradise as it is possible to be in the British Isles, with more sunshine hours than anyone else enjoys. There are no tall mountains, but the rocks around the coast are as dramatic as you'll find anywhere. There are no extensive moorlands, but you'll forget that as you walk round the open heathery headlands. The islands may be small in extent, but the eye is deceived and readily imagines vast panoramas and awesome seascapes. Views to the sea take in jagged rocks that have ripped many a keel and wrecked many a ship. The islands are clothed in colourful flowers, both cultivated

and wild, and attract a rich bird life, including native breeding species and seasonal migrants. And always, there is the sea.

The Isles of Scilly form the smallest of Britain's Areas of Outstanding Natural Beauty, and their historic shores have been designated as Heritage Coast. The surrounding sea is protected as a Marine Park of great biodiversity. Archaeological remains abound, not only on the islands, but also submerged beneath the sea. The Isles of Scilly are special, revealing their secrets and charms to those who walk the headlands, sail from island to island, and take the time to observe the sights, sounds and scents of the landscape. While the walks in this guidebook could be completed in as little as a week, a fortnight would allow a much more leisurely appreciation of the islands, and leave memories that will last for a lifetime.

Granite is the bedrock of the Isles of Scilly, seen at its best around Peninnis Head (Walk 3)

LOCATION

The Isles of Scilly lie 45km (28 miles) west of Land's End: a position that ensures they are omitted from most maps of Britain, or shown only as an inset. There are five inhabited islands and about fifty other areas that local people would call islands, as well as a hundred more rocks, and more again at low water. The islands are not part of Cornwall, perish the thought, but a self-administering unit; you could think of this as the smallest county in Britain (see www.scilly.gov.uk). The total landmass is a mere 16km² (6¼ square miles). The waters around the Isles of Scilly, extending as far as the 50m (165ft) submarine contour, form a Marine Park of around 125km² (50 square miles). Despite the small area of the islands, walkers can enjoy up to about 80km (50 miles) of truly remarkable routes around one of Britain's most charming and intensely interesting landscapes.

GEOLOGY

The geology of the Isles of Scilly can be summed up in one word – granite. The islands are the south-western extremity of a deep-seated granite mass, or batholith, that reaches the surface of the earth around Dartmoor, Bodmin Moor and Land's End. Granite is the bedrock of the Isles of Scilly, and it breaks down to form a stony, sandy or gritty soil, as well as bright white sandy beaches. In some places around the coast and occasionally inland, the granite forms blocky cliffs and tors, rounded boulders or tilted slabs that have such a rough texture that they provide excellent grip for walkers. In other places chemical weathering of less stable minerals within the granite causes the rock to crumble, or peel away in layers. As a building material, granite has been used for centuries, but only in relatively recent times has it been possible to split the rock into squared blocks more suitable for substantial buildings.

While the Isles of Scilly escaped the Ice Age that affected much of Britain, it didn't escape the permafrost conditions that pertained south of the ice sheets, breaking up the granite tors and forming a stony, sandy soil. Nor did the islands fare too well as the ice began to melt and sea levels began to rise. It is thought that Scilly became separated from the rest of Britain around 10,000 years ago. It may well have been a single landmass for a while, but a combination of rising sea levels and coastal erosion produced the current pattern of five islands and a bewildering number of rocks and reefs. Before the arrival of the first settlers, it was no doubt a wild and wooded place.

ANCIENT HISTORY

Arthurian legend points to the Isles of Scilly as the last remnants of the lost land of Lyonesse; but while a submerged landscape does exist around the islands, it was never Lyonesse. In

The Inisidgen Upper Burial Chamber on the coast of St Mary's is 4000 years old (Walk 3)

1752 the Cornish antiquarian William Borlase discovered and recorded submerged field systems on the tidal flats near Samson. It seems that the first settlers were Neolithic, but a more comprehensive settlement of the islands came in the Bronze Age, up to 4000 years ago. Some splendid ritual standing stones and stoutly constructed burial chambers remain from this time, and excavations have revealed skeletons, cremated remains and a host of artefacts. When the Romans began their occupation of Britain 2000 years ago, criss-crossing the land with straight roads, settlement patterns on the Isles of Scilly were in huddled formations, as witnessed today on Halangy Down and Nornour. No doubt the Romans traded with the islands, as coins have been discovered, but it seems they established

no lasting presence. In later centuries the Isles of Scilly attracted Christian hermits, leaving some of the islands blessed with the names of saints. That great seafaring race, the Vikings, also visited the islands. From time to time the Isles of Scilly have been a haven for pirates, their retreat every now and then smashed by the authorities of the day. In the 11th century over one hundred pirates were beheaded in a single day on Tresco!

LATER HISTORY

A Benedictine priory was founded on Tresco in the 12th century, and Henry I granted the island to Tavistock Abbey. By the 14th century the islands became part of the Duchy of Cornwall and Edward III gave them to the Black Prince, who was made

The remains of a 12th-century Benedictine priory at the Abbey Garden on Tresco (Walk 10)

the Duke of Cornwall. In the 16th century Governor Francis Godolphin was granted the lease of the islands by Elizabeth I. Godolphin built the eight-pointed Star Castle above the harbour on St Mary's. During the Civil War, in the middle of the 17th century, Prince Charles (later King Charles II) stayed briefly at the Star Castle. Towards the end of the Civil War the islands were occupied by disgruntled Royalists who launched pirate raids on passing ships, causing the Dutch to send a fleet of ships to deal with the problem. An English fleet intercepted the Dutch, preventing wholesale destruction on the islands, and thereby gaining the final surrender of the Royalist force.

The 18th century was a time of great poverty on the islands, but despite their remoteness John Wesley visited them in the course of his preaching around the British Isles. Shipbuilding became an important occupation late in the 18th century and continued well into the 19th century. In the early 19th century the Godolphin family allowed their lease on the Isles of Scilly to lapse, so that they reverted to the Duchy of Cornwall. In 1834 Augustus Smith from Hertfordshire took over the lease of the islands as Lord Proprietor, and developed Tresco in particular, building the Abbey House as his residence and establishing the Abbey Garden.

The successful export of flowers from the islands dates from the middle of the 19th century and has enjoyed mixed fortunes. During 1918 the Dorrien-Smith family gave up the lease on all the islands except Tresco. While fortifications on St Mary's were strengthened in the First World War, the islands escaped lightly. During the Second World War, however, there was a lot more activity around the islands, as submarines and warships played deadly hide and seek in the waters, and several warplanes were stationed there.

RECENT HISTORY

In a sudden magnanimous gesture in 1949, the Duchy of Cornwall offered the sale of the freehold on most properties occupied by sitting tenants in Hugh Town. The Isles of Scilly were designated as an Area of Outstanding Natural Beauty in 1975, www.ios-aonb.info. The Duchy leases all its uninhabited islands and unfarmed wilderness land to the Isles of Scilly Wildlife trust, www.ios-wildlifetrust.org.uk. The annual rent is one daffodil! The Trust manages this land for conservation and recreation, safeguarding habitats for flora and fauna, while maintaining the network of footpaths over the land. The designation of a Marine Park to conserve the surrounding sea bed and marine life was another important development. The infrastructure of the islands continues to develop and tourism is an increasingly important industry, but always with due regard to the environment and the conservation of nature.

These brief notes can only give the barest outline of the islands'

The Isles of Scilly have a most colourful
and turbulent history and heritage (Walk 10)

history, which has been turbulent and colourful and makes an interesting and absorbing study. Be sure to visit the Isles of Scilly Museum, www.iosmuseum.org, in Hugh Town on St Mary's for a more thorough grounding and to obtain further information.

GETTING TO THE ISLES OF SCILLY

By Road: The A30 road is the main transport artery through the south-west, pushing through Devon and Cornwall, around Dartmoor and over Bodmin Moor, to terminate abruptly at Land's End. Motorists will have to abandon their vehicles at airports such as Exeter, Newquay or Land's End for short flights to Scilly, or at Penzance for the ferry. Cars cannot be taken to the islands, nor are they necessary, so enquire about secure long-term car parking, either in Penzance or at the airports. National Express buses serve Penzance from London, Plymouth, Birmingham and Scotland. Bear in mind, if travelling on weekends, that there are no flights and rarely any ferries to or from the Isles of Scilly on Sundays.

By Rail: The rail network terminates at Penzance, served by daily Cross Country trains, www.crosscountrytrains.co.uk, direct from Manchester and Birmingham, or, with a simple change at Birmingham, services operate from as far away as Leeds, Newcastle, Edinburgh, Glasgow and Aberdeen. First Great Western trains run to Penzance daily from London Paddington, www.firstgreatwestern.co.uk.

Combined rail/sail deals are available through the Isles of Scilly Travel Centre. Transfers can be arranged between Penzance railway station and Land's End airport, if you chose to fly and enquire while booking your flight. A short walk around the harbour from the railway station leads to the far quay where the *Scillonian III* sails for the Isles of Scilly. Bear in mind, if travelling on weekends, that there are no flights and rarely any ferries to or from the Isles of Scilly on Sundays.

By Ship: The *Scillonian III* is a fine little ship of 1000 tonnes, sailing once each way between Penzance and St Mary's from Monday to Saturday throughout the year. In the high season there are usually two journeys on Saturdays. Observe the regulations for carrying luggage, which should always be labelled with your destination, and clearly labelled with the name of the particular island you are visiting. Luggage can be conveyed to your accommodation in Hugh Town, but be sure to follow instructions to avail of this service. The journey usually takes 2¾ hours. It is customary for the ship's whistle to sound half an hour before each sailing to keep you on your toes! Bad weather can cause the schedule to be altered in the winter months. For details contact the Isles of Scilly Travel Centre, tel 0845 7105555; www.islesofscilly-travel.co.uk

By Aeroplane: All flights to St Mary's are operated by Skybus,

Penzance harbour in Cornwall, from where the Scillonia III sails to the islands

www.skybus.co.uk, using Twin Otter or Islander aircraft. Flights are available from Exeter, Newquay and Land's End. Frequency is generally higher on the shorter flights, with those from Land's End taking only 15 minutes each way. There are no flights on Sundays. Schedules and prices can be checked with the Isles of Scilly Travel Centre, tel 0845 7105555, www.islesofscilly-travel.co.uk. Minibuses meet incoming flights and will take passengers directly to their accommodation on St Mary's.

GETTING AROUND THE ISLES OF SCILLY

Buses and Taxis: A regular Community Bus service operates in a circuit around St Mary's, as well as minibus and vintage bus tours around the island. There are also a handful of taxis, should you need to get to any place in a hurry. Most of the buses start from beside a little park near the Town Hall in the middle of Hugh Town, though services can also be checked at the Tourist Information Centre. There is an airport minibus service that operates from in front of the chemist's shop a short way inland from The Quay. The off-islands are small enough to walk around on foot and walkers don't really need any other form of transport. If choosing an accommodation base on one of the off-islands, the proprietor may be able to meet you at the quayside with a vehicle and assist with transferring luggage, but ask if this is possible when booking.

St Mary's Boatmen's Association: Run on a co-operative basis, the Association runs several launches from Hugh Town on St Mary's to the off-islands of St Agnes, Bryher, Tresco and St Martin's. Launches to Bryher may also drop passengers at the uninhabited island of Samson on request. Details of services run by the Association, plus a wealth of cruises, are advertised on notice boards on The Quay at Hugh Town, as well as at the quaysides on the off-islands. Details can also be obtained from the Tourist Information Centre. The Association operates a small ticket kiosk on the Old Quay at Hugh Town. There are more ferries and cruises to more places in the high season than in

Have a look at the noticeboards on The Quay at Hugh Town for details of trips (Walk 1)

the winter months. Bear in mind that the onset of stormy weather can lead to the sudden cancellation of all boat services around the islands. St Mary's Boatmen's Association can be contacted at Rose Cottage, The Strand, St Mary's, Isles of Scilly, TR21 0PT, tel 01720 423999, www.scillyboating. co.uk. Other services to and from the off-islands are operated by St Agnes Boating, tel 01720 422704, www. stagnesboating.co.uk; Bryher Boat Services (Bryher and Tresco), tel 01720 422886, www.bryherboats.co.uk; and St Martin's Boat Services, tel 01720 422814, mobile 07831 585365.

BOAT TRIPS

Quite apart from using boats as a means of access to islands and walks, why not enjoy a series of boat trips? Some trips are operated by the St Mary's Boatmen's Association, on their large launches, while others are run using smaller boats, which usually limit their passenger numbers to twelve. Classic trips run by the St Mary's Boatmen's Association include tours around the Western Rocks, Norrard Rocks, St Helen's and Teän, the Eastern Isles, and a complete circuit around St Mary's. There are Seabird Specials for bird-watchers, historical tours, evening visits to St Agnes and St Martin's for supper, and the chance to follow the popular Gig Races in the high season.

At some point during your visit to the Isles of Scilly, be sure to witness the evening Gig Races. This is the main spectator sport on the islands, when teams row furiously along a measured 2km (1¼ mile) course from Nut Rock, across the stretch of sea known as 'The Road', to The Quay at Hugh Town. Women's teams compete on Wednesday evenings, while men's teams compete on Friday evenings. Boats generally leave The Quay at 1930 on those evenings. World Championships take place over the May Bank Holiday.

Do you sample some of these boat trips to broaden your experience and enjoyment of the islands, and you should make every effort to include as many of the remote islands and rock groups as possible.

TOURIST INFORMATION AND ACCOMMODATION

The Tourist Information Centre in Hugh Town on St Mary's can provide plenty of information about accommodation, pubs, restaurants, transport and attractions throughout the Isles of Scilly. Between April and October some 75,000 people stay on the islands, and an additional 25,000 people make day trips. In August the islands can run out of beds for visitors, so advance booking is always recommended. All the islands except Tresco have campsites, and these can fill too.

There are abundant self-catering cottages and chalets, as well as plenty of B&B establishments and

Accommodation around the islands ranges from luxury hotels to basic campsites

guesthouses. There are nine hotels; six of them around Hugh Town on St Mary's and one on each of the off-islands except St Agnes. For full details and a full colour brochure contact the Isles of Scilly Tourist Information Centre, Porthcressa Bank, St Mary's, Isles of Scilly TR21 0LW, tel 01720 424031, www.visitislesofscilly.co.uk. Other websites containing useful information and news include www.scillyonline.co.uk and www.scillytoday.com. It is worth listening to Radio Scilly on 107.9fm while you are staying on the islands, www.facebook.com/radioscilly.

A lot of time and effort can be spent trying to tie ferry and flight schedules into accommodation availability on the islands in the high season, and there may be a need to spend a night before or after your trip at Penzance on the mainland. Arrangements can be simplified by letting Isles of Scilly Inclusive Holidays handle all your requirements in a complete package, tel 01720 422200, www.islesofscillyholidays.co.uk.

MAPS OF THE ISLES OF SCILLY

The Isles of Scilly could be explored easily enough without using maps, as the total land area is only 16km^2 (6¼ square miles), but mapless visitors would miss a great deal along the way. Detailed maps reveal alternative routes and other options to the walks in this book. Dozens of near and distant features can be identified in view, and access to all the relevant placenames is literally at your fingertips.

The following maps of the islands are available in a variety of scales and styles. Ordnance Survey grid references indicate the starting point of each walk throughout this guidebook.

Ordnance Survey 1:25,000 Explorer 101 – Isles of Scilly. This map gives the most accurate depiction of the Isles of Scilly on one large sheet, including all the rocks and reefs that make up this complex group, along with a wealth of interesting and amazing placenames.

Ordnance Survey 1:50,000 Landranger 203 – Land's End, The Lizard & Isles of Scilly. This map shows the Isles of Scilly as an inset. The map offers little detail of the islands and is not particularly recommended detailed exploration, though it is a useful general map and worth having if you are also considering walking around neighbouring Land's End and The Lizard in Cornwall.

Free leaflets containing maps of all or some of the islands can be collected from the Tourist Information Centre or picked up from other locations. Some will prove useful, others less useful, and many of them exist to highlight a variety of services and attractions around the islands. Marine navigation charts are for those who sail as well as walk, or for serious marine studies.

The maps in this guidebook are extracted from the Ordnance Survey 1:25,000 map and an overlay shows the walking routes. A few of the maps aren't of walking routes, but show groups of small islands and rocks that can be visited on boat trips and are covered by short descriptive chapters.

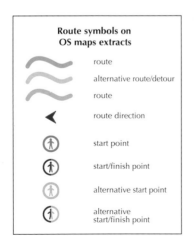

Route symbols on OS maps extracts

≈ route

≈ alternative route/detour

≈ route

◄ route direction

🚶 start point

🚶 start/finish point

🚶 alternative start point

🚶 alternative start/finish point

There are also a few small-scale plans, showing greater detail of Hugh Town, The Garrison and the amazing Tresco Abbey Garden.

THE WALKS

None of the walks on the Isles of Scilly could really be described as difficult. The only way anyone could make them difficult is by rushing through them, which surely defeats the purpose of exploring the islands when there is so much of interest to see. The walks make use of a network of paths, mostly along the coast, but sometimes inland too. They may also follow tracks and roads, but those roads are likely to be free of traffic. Sensible precautions include wearing stout shoes, possibly boots, when walking along uneven or rocky paths, and carrying a set of waterproofs in case of rain. When stormy weather whips up the waves, you can get drenched from salt spray. In any case it is always advisable to proceed with caution whenever walking close to breaking waves; there is always the chance that the next wave will break considerably higher. Unprotected cliffs also need to be approached with caution, especially in high winds or blustery conditions. The sun can be exceptionally strong, so if you burn easily then be sure to keep your skin covered, either with light-coloured, lightweight, comfortable polycotton clothing or a high-factor sunscreen. A good sun hat is also useful, but ensure

it is one that ties on so that it won't be blown away and lost at sea!

The walks included in this guidebook allow an exploration of the coastlines of the five inhabited islands, as well as some of the smaller islands. With the aid of cruises, walkers can also enjoy close-up views of the Eastern Isles, Norrard Rocks, Western Rocks and even the solitary pillar of the Bishop Rock Lighthouse. It all depends how long you stay on the islands and how much you wish to see. Walkers in a hurry could complete all these walks in a week, but two weeks would give a more leisurely chance to explore and include a number of boat trips. Better still, make two or three trips throughout the year to appreciate the changing seasons.

By no means do these walks exhaust all the possibilities for exploring the islands, and there are just as many quiet and unfrequented paths left for you to discover. Apart from the walking route descriptions, there are also short descriptions of small islands that might well be visited out of interest, but where the walking potential is really quite limited.

GUIDED WALKS

Your visit to the Isles of Scilly can be enhanced by taking part in a series of guided walks that are available largely in the high season. These are walks led by knowledgeable local people, with a specific emphasis on wildlife and heritage. By joining one of these walks

None of the walks around the Isles of Scilly could really be described as difficult

you have a chance to keep up to date with what is happening in the natural world. Flowers bloom and fade, birds come and go on their migrations, and a good guide will explain what is currently happening around the islands. Furthermore, there is a chance to ask specific questions on the spot. For details of guided walks, enquire at the Tourist Information Office or the Isles of Scilly Wildlife Trust Office. There are also specific wildlife cruises – some operating during the day and others departing at dusk, depending on what is likely to be sighted.

Island Wildlife Tours offers visitors the chance to appreciate the wildlife around the Isles of Scilly, in the company of a resident naturalist and ornithologist. Contact Will Wagstaff, 42 Sallyport, St Mary's, Isles of Scilly, TR21 0JE, tel 01720 422212, www.islandwildflowertours.co.uk.

Scilly Walks explores the ancient history and heritage of the Isles of Scilly in the company of a resident archaeologist. Contact Katharine Sawyer, Alegria, High Lanes, St Mary's, Isles of Scilly, TR21 0NW, tel 01720 423326, www.scillywalks.co.uk.

Walk Scilly is the Isles of Scilly walking festival, taking place in April each year, offering a variety of walks and evening events, organised and led by island residents with outstanding knowledge. Contact the Tourist Information Centre for details.

ISLAND FLOWERS

There are two broad classes of flowers on the Isles of Scilly: those grown for sale and shipment to the mainland, and those that grow in the wild. Bear in mind that wild flowers do creep into the cultivated flower fields, and some of the cultivated flowers have a habit of hopping out into the wilds! The flower industry started in 1868 when the tenant of Rocky Hill Farm on St Mary's packed some flowers into a box and sent them to Covent Garden. Within a few years there were fields of daffodils and narcissus being grown. Visitors expecting to see fields of golden blooms will be disappointed, as the flowers are cut before they bloom. A field of wonderful blooms is technically a failed crop! To protect the tiny flower fields from wind and salt spray, tall, dense windbreak hedgerows are planted. Hedging species include pittosporum, euonymus and veronica, though there are also tall shelter belts of long-established Monterey and lodgepole pines. There are flower farms on each of the inhabited islands, and some specialise in posting fresh flowers to British destinations on request. There are also bulb farms, offering a selection of hardy bulbs that are more likely to survive the journey home.

Wild flowers number around 700 species around the Isles of Scilly, making any attempt to list them here a rather pointless exercise. There are some plants that are peculiar to the islands, either growing nowhere else in Britain or being sub-species of plants that are found elsewhere in Britain. Almost 250 species are included on the Isles of Scilly Wildlife Trust Flower Checklist, which is an invaluable leaflet to carry around the islands, along with a good field guide to flowering plants. Common plants include bracken, heather and gorse on most open uncultivated areas, with bulbous cushions of thrift on many cliffs and rocky areas.

Perhaps one of the most startling escapees from the flower fields are the large agapanthus blooms, which now decorate many sand dunes, growing among the marram grass. Fleshy mesembryanthemums, or Hottentot figs also creep through the dunes. The tropical Tresco Abbey Garden contains 3000 species from around the world, making that one small area alone a very special place for more careful study!

ISLAND BIRDS

The Isles of Scilly are renowned for their bird life, and while resident breeding species may be few, the islands are an important landfall for many more migrant species in the spring and autumn. Anything up to 400 species of birds have been recorded around the islands, but this includes some extremely uncommon birds that somehow find themselves well off their usual migratory routes. Almost 150 species are included on the Isles of Scilly Wildlife Trust Bird Checklist, which is an invaluable leaflet to carry around the islands, along with a good field guide to birds.

Seabirds are, of course, plentiful. Herring gulls, greater and lesser black-backed gulls and kittiwakes are fairly common. Four species of terns are present, including Arctic terns on their amazing round-the-world migrations. Cormorants and shags frequent isolated rocks and cliff ledges, easily spotted because of their habit of holding their wings outstretched for long periods. By taking a wildlife cruise you can see great 'rafts' of shags far out to

Lovely to look at, but a field of flowers in full bloom is technically a failed crop!

Gulls are everywhere around the islands, but there are plenty of rare birds to see

sea, and maybe also smaller 'rafts' of Manx shearwaters.

Auks include guillemots and razorbills, sleeker and more slender than the comical puffins that are eagerly awaited each spring by birdwatchers. During the breeding season male puffins have rainbow-hued bills, used for courtship display, aggression against other males, and for digging

burrows. Like the Manx shearwater, puffins nesting on dry land live in mortal fear of gulls. Storm petrels and fulmar petrels nest in isolated places, out on remote rocky ledges or on the island sanctuary of Annet. With their amazing flying dives, gannets provide the most startling feeding display of any of the seabirds. While most people imagine them spearing fish with their bills, they actually seem to catch fish while swimming back to the surface. The inter-tidal flats, especially around the shallow lagoon in the middle of the Isles of Scilly, attract a host of waders. Piping oystercatchers probe the sands, while turnstones, naturally, prefer to look beneath stones in search of food. Sanderlings, sand pipers, whimbrel and ringed plovers may also be seen on the sands, with rock pipits preferring the higher, drier regions of the beaches. 'Seabird 2000' was a comprehensive count of all seabird species around Britain that took place during the years 1999–2001. Counting the birds around the Isles of Scilly involved volunteers visiting most of the exposed rocks around the islands.

While there are no great freshwater lakes on the Isles of Scilly, there are several small pools and ponds. Many of these attract waterfowl and some have been equipped with bird hides to aid observation. A few uncommon species of herons have been spotted around the islands. Snipe, redshanks and greenshanks are attracted to water, along with moorhens, ducks, geese and swans. Water rails are commonly spotted, and it is worth looking out for little egrets in the autumn. Reeds and willows surround many of the pools, so a variety of warblers, wagtails and flycatchers find them a favourable habitat. Kingfishers, though highly uncommon, often startle birdwatchers with a sudden flash of iridescent blue.

There are plenty of birds to be spotted around the fields and hedgerows.

Wrens, though tiny, are really quite numerous. Blackbirds and thrushes, swallows and martins, finches and tits all favour these habitats, while more open spaces may feature redwing and fieldfare. Stonechats prefer spiky gorse bushes. Cuckoos are often heard earlier in the Isles of Scilly than mainland Britain, and the poor rock pipits often find themselves raising cuckoo chicks. Birds of prey include kestrels, merlins, peregrines and hobbies. Birds that you shouldn't expect to see include owls, magpies and woodpeckers, but occasionally a true rarity blows in from distant climes. For up-to-date details of birds around the islands, go to www.scilly-birding.co.uk

ISLAND ANIMALS

There are very few wild animals to spot around the Isles of Scilly, but one peculiar little creature is the Scilly shrew, which is a distinct variation from its mainland cousins. Animals that have been introduced to the islands include hedgehogs, which are present only on St Mary's, and slow worms, only on Bryher.

MARINE PARK WILDLIFE

Although the waters around the Isles of Scilly are protected as a Marine Park, few visitors are aware of the importance of this habitat. Four special areas within the Marine Park have been identified. The Western Rocks are described as super-exposed and can support only the hardiest communities of plants and animals. St Agnes and Annet have pebbly sea-beds around them, supporting a range of rare seaweeds. The east coast of St Mary's has sheltered bedrock providing a habitat for solitary corals, branched sponges, delicate sea fans and other similar species. Despite their 'roots' and plant-like appearance, these species are actually animals. The flats around Samson, Tresco and St Martin's are the shallowest waters around the Isles of Scilly, with rich communities of seaweeds and animals. An abundance of hard-shelled molluscs include scallops,

limpets, razor shells, cowries and periwinkles. Sea urchins are numerous, but live in deep water and only occasionally are their shells cast ashore. Crabs and lobsters are common.

There are a surprising number of large mammals in the sea around the islands. Grey or Atlantic seals can be observed resting on remote shores and tidal ledges. Dolphins and porpoises are occasionally spotted around the islands, but more often favour the open ocean, as do more rarely spotted pilot and killer whales. The chances of seeing marine species are of course increased by taking one of the wildlife cruises advertised around the islands.

Seals can sometimes be approached closely on boat trips around the rocks

FISHING

Fishing is now a minor occupation around the Isles of Scilly, but it is interesting to see what species are caught. Dogfish and rays are present, and their egg cases can be found on the shores. Plaice, sole, skate, mackerel, cod, monkfish, pollock, turbot, mullet and hake are all caught. There are conger eels and squid, and every so often peculiar species such as marlin and sea horses make their way into these waters. Commercial shrimping and prawning is restricted to three months in the summer. Very occasionally huge basking sharks are seen, their enormous mouths filtering the water for the tiniest marine organisms. These sharks used to be hunted for the oil in their livers, and became something of a rarity, though they seem to be on the increase again. Most of the fish caught commercially are packed away to the mainland, but local fishermen do supply some of the hotels, guesthouses and restaurants with fresh catches. Crabs and lobsters are lifted, but traditional pots have been replaced by plastic ones.

ISLES OF SCILLY WILDLIFE TRUST

The Isles of Scilly Environment Trust was formed in 1985, and by 1987 had secured a 99-year lease on all the un-farmed wilderness land owned by the Duchy of Cornwall. This includes substantial areas of St Mary's, St Agnes and Gugh, Bryher and St Martin's, as well as all the uninhabited islands and rocks. Tresco, which is leased to Robert Dorrien-Smith, is not managed by the Trust. The organisation became the Isles of Scilly Wildlife Trust in 2001.

The remit of the Trust is wide-ranging, but basically encompasses maintaining a balance between wildlife conservation and recreation. Staff maintain the footpath network on the islands, and have an ongoing programme to control bracken and gorse and to replenish the native tree cover. Visitors can help by contributing to a tree-planting scheme. Ancient monuments need to be cleared of scrub and protected from damage, important nesting sites for birds need to be kept free from interference, and constant monitoring of the environment is necessary. It all takes time and it costs money.

Visitors to the Isles of Scilly are invited to become Friends of Scilly. It is also worth visiting the Trust office in Hugh Town, where a wealth of interesting publications can be purchased. Staff also occasionally lead walks and wildlife trips. Information can be obtained on The Quay in Hugh Town, or from the Isles of Scilly Wildlife Trust, Trenoweth, St Mary's, Isles of Scilly, TR21 0NS. Tel 01720 422153; www.ios-wildlifetrust.org.uk

THE DUCHY OF CORNWALL

Many visitors to the Isles of Scilly wonder about the role of the Duchy of Cornwall, since mention is made of this body virtually everywhere. The Duchy is a series of estates, by no means all in Cornwall, but throughout Britain, which exist to provide an income to the heir to the throne.

Established in the 14th century, the extent of land controlled by the Duchy has varied through the centuries, but has always included the Isles of Scilly. As the islands' landlord, the Duchy has always raised its revenue through the sale of leases and collection of rents on the land. Some of the earliest rents were paid in the form of salted puffins!

It is probably through the influence of Prince Charles that the Duchy has an increased awareness of the environmental and aesthetic value of the land in its control. Information boards can be studied in the harbour waiting room at Hugh

Town, outlining the role of the Duchy in the life of the islands. The Duchy office is at Hugh House on the Garrison above Hugh Town on St Mary's. Members of the Royal Family have occasionally used a secretive little bungalow nearby for informal holidays. Its location used to be jealously guarded by islanders, but now they gleefully point it out to visitors!

PLAN OF THIS GUIDE

The plan of this guidebook is simple. The first few walks are on St Mary's, taking in a town trail around Hugh Town, a stroll around The Garrison, then more extended walks around the coast and along the nature trails of St Mary's. The rest of the islands are visited in a roughly clockwise direction, with Gugh and St Agnes being explored in turn.

Short chapters describe some of the smaller islands and groups of islets and rocks; and as visits must be on boat trips, no walking routes are offered. Thus, the guidebook works its way around Annet and the Western Rocks, Samson, Bryher and the Norrard Rocks. Tresco and the little islands of St Helen's and Teän give way to St Martin's and the Eastern Isles, bringing this delightful tour around the Isles of Scilly full circle. Although of limited extent, it takes a lot of time to explore.

SAFETY MATTERS

It is highly unlikely that anyone could get lost in the Isles of Scilly, although it might be possible to get on the wrong ferry and land on the wrong island, or become marooned on an uninhabited island! Apart from that, while walkers may occasionally be unsure exactly which headland or bay they have reached, they cannot be much more than an hour's walk from wherever they started.

Apart from minor cuts and grazes, accidents are unlikely, though care needs to be taken around cliff coasts, and special care needs to be taken in any case while walking beside the sea. If tempted to walk along beaches, or visit rocks and islets at low tide, always ensure that there is an easy escape route before the tide flows in again. Tide times can be checked locally, or at www.tidetimes.org.uk.

In the event of accident, the police, fire service, ambulance or coastguard can be summoned by dialling 999 (the European 112 works also). Be sure to give a full account of the nature of the accident, as well as your own contact details, so that the emergency services can stay in touch with you. A little forethought will ensure an accident-free trip.

WALK 1
Hugh Town Trail

Start	Rat Island on The Quay, SV 902 109
Distance	2.5km (1½ miles)

The main settlement on St Mary's used to be Old Town, but during the construction of the defences around the Garrison, people drifted onto the narrow neck of land between the harbour and Porth Cressa, and Hugh Town grew throughout the 17th century. Hugh Town is by far the largest settlement on the Isles of Scilly. In a sense it is the islands' capital, even though it only has the appearance of a small town or large village.

A stroll around Hugh Town is something you should complete at the start of any exploration of the Isles of Scilly, so that you become aware of the islands' greatest range of services, and know where to find things and how the place operates. Hugh Town, for all its small size, is packed with history and heritage and all kinds of interesting corners. Most buildings are built of granite, the bedrock of the islands, and they stand cheek by jowl on a narrow neck of land between the Garrison and the larger part of St Mary's. Take special note of all the slide shows that are offered in the evenings in the high season. Knowledgeable local people present these talks; people with a passion for the history, heritage, flowers and wildlife of the islands.

The Quay is an obvious place to start this walk. Those who reach the Isles of Scilly using the *Scillonian III* place their feet on this stout granite quay before walking anywhere else in the islands. The Quay connects Rat Island to Hugh Town, with the Old Quay, closest to town, dating from 1603.

Don't rush straight into town. The Harbourside Hotel sits on **Rat Island**, offering food and drink here at the start. The ferry waiting room beside the hotel is full of informative panels about the history and natural history of the islands, and these are well worth a few minutes of study. The Isles of Scilly Wildlife Trust operates a small

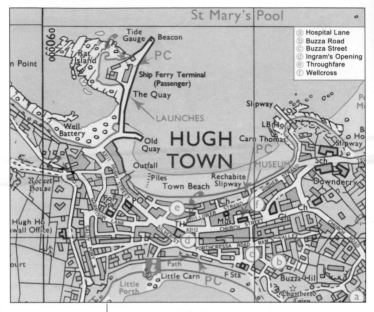

visitor centre full of interesting information. Be sure to look inside.

While following The Quay towards town, take note of all the notice boards advertising ferries to the off-islands, wildlife cruises, evening cruises and all the rest. There is a small stone kiosk on the **Old Quay** where tickets can be obtained for the off-islands launches and cruises run by St Mary's Boatmen's Association. For most other cruises and trips, either book in advance or pay on board. Ten o'clock in the morning is the busiest time in high season, when everyone flocks down to the quays for their tickets and the launches take their first eager passengers to each of the off-islands.

Turn left at the **Mermaid Inn** and walk along **Hugh Street.** The Pilot's Gig Restaurant is off to the right, but continue straight onwards, passing the Atlantic Hotel, which is on the left. Hugh Street is like a canyon of granite and it is fortunate that space is limited, so few vehicles use it. The **Post Office** stands beside a rugged granite arch and bears a stone marked 'VR 1897'. A fine granite terrace of houses continues on that side of the street, while the Isles of Scilly Steamship Company office is on the left. A group of gift shops are clustered around a road junction. The Bishop & Wolf is a bar and restaurant to the right, but keep left to reach a more open square. The **Town Hall** stands to the right, carrying a date-stone of 1887, and the small green space in the middle of Hugh Town serves as the town park. Taxis, small tour buses and a vintage bus may be parked here, should anyone fancy a quick spin around St Mary's along its rather limited road network.

Keep left of the little park, following **Lower Strand Street**. The **Custom House** is to the left, and the Star of the Sea Catholic Church is to the right. A toilet block stands beside a short promenade path, where there are fine views across the harbour, while inland, shops give way to a terrace of houses. The **Lifeboat Station** is tucked under the granite tor of Carn Thomas and is served by a short path. If you follow it, then you have to return afterwards. The latest lifeboat is called *The Whiteheads* and is usually moored out on the harbour.

The road called **Higher Strand** climbs uphill, but turn sharply right at the top to discover the Isles of Scilly Wildlife Trust office. They may have a series of wildlife walks or cruises planned, so ask for details. Just around the corner is the **Parish Church** of St Mary the Virgin, dating from 1835, and a cylindrical granite tower, which was once a windmill, can be seen on Buzza Hill. Walk straight down into town along Church Street. St Mary's Hall Hotel is on the right, as well as the **Methodist Church.** There may be a notice posted at the church detailing evening slide shows. The Bell Rock Hotel is on the left.

The **Isles of Scilly Museum** stands on the right, in a rather faceless modern building. Don't be put off by the façade, as the interior is absolutely packed with interest. There are plenty of items relating to the history and heritage of the islands, as well as exhibits detailing the flora and fauna. Leaving the museum, the Church Hall is on the right, and again there may be a notice detailing evening slide shows. A terrace of granite guesthouses leads back to the little park and the **Town Hall.**

Turn left to reach Porthcressa Bank and the Tourist Information Centre, for a view of **Porth Cressa Beach**. Walk back towards town and turn left along **Silver Street,** behind the Town Hall, and head back into the middle of Hugh Town. Turn left at Mumford's, where books, maps, postcards and the like can be bought.

Follow **Garrison Lane** uphill. The police station is on the right, but turn left along **Sallyport.** Look for a sign above a passageway marked 'Garrison Through Archway' to be led through a housing block and under the Garrison Walls by way of the low-roofed Sallyport. Turn left along a narrow road to reach **Hugh House**, the Duchy of Cornwall office, facing the **Garden Battery**. Enjoy a view over the rooftops of Hugh Town, appreciating just how compact the little town really is.

Follow the road past the **Higher Battery**, then walk down to the Powder Magazine Exhibition to learn about the fortifications of the Garrison. Turn left up to the **Star Castle Hotel**, which can be visited by non-residents. While walking back downhill afterwards, pass through an old archway dated 1742 at **Gatehouse Cottage.**

Walk downhill past Tregarthen's Hotel, which was founded by Captain Tregarthen. He used to bring passengers to the Isles of Scilly 150 years ago, whenever he brought supplies from the mainland. There was a catch; his guests couldn't leave the islands until he went back to the mainland for more supplies! Turn left below the hotel to return to the harbour where the town trail started.

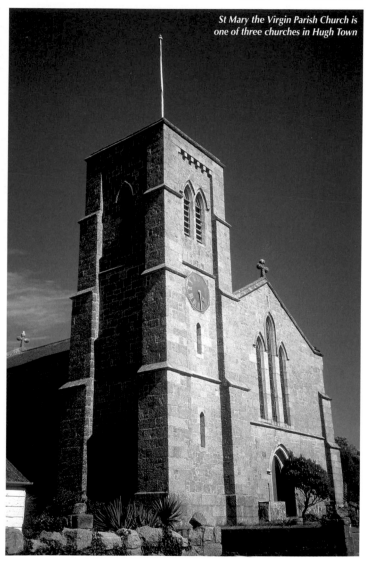

St Mary the Virgin Parish Church is one of three churches in Hugh Town

FACILITIES IN HUGH TOWN

Most services and facilities on the Isles of Scilly are concentrated around Hugh Town. If you can't find what you need here, then you probably won't find it anywhere on the islands. Anything else must be brought from the mainland!

- There are a few **hotels** around Hugh Town, as well as the largest concentration of **guest houses**, **bed and breakfast** establishments and **self-catering** accommodation in the islands.

- The only two **banks** available in the Isles of Scilly are Barclays and Lloyds (the latter with an ATM) and both are in Hugh Town. The **Co-op**, as well as a few other shops and pubs, offers a cashback service.

- There is a **post office**, **chemist** and **newsagent**, as well as a number of **shops** selling provisions, crafts and souvenirs.

- Although several **pubs**, **restaurants** and **cafés** are available, in the high season it is wise to book in advance for meals.

- There is an interesting **museum** in town, tel 01720 422337, www.iosmuseum.org.

- The **police station**, **hospital** and all administrative services for the Isles of Scilly are located around Hugh Town.

- **Churches** include St Mary the Virgin (Church of England), Our Lady Star of the Sea Catholic Church and the Methodist Church.

- **Toilets** are located on The Quay, on The Strand and at Porth Cressa.

- **Tour buses** that make circuits around St Mary's, as well as taxis, run from clearly marked stands in the centre of Hugh Town, near the Town Hall.

- **Ferries** to the off-islands all depart from The Quay, along with **cruise trips** and the **Scillonian III** ferry to Penzance.

WALK 2
The Garrison Wall

Start	Garrison Gate in Hugh Town, SV 901 106
Distance	2.5km (1½ miles)

The promontory to the west of Hugh Town is almost completely encircled by a stout, granite defensive wall bristling with batteries. The Garrison was developed in stages over three centuries, but the most significant starting date is 1593, when Governor Francis Godolphin built the eight-pointed Star Castle. Additional walls and batteries were built around the promontory, with more appearing during the Civil War. The Garrison held out as a Royalist stronghold until 1651. Other islands holding out to the bitter end included Jersey, in the Channel Islands, and Inishbofin, off the west coast of Ireland. The Garrison came to resemble its present form during restructuring associated with the Wars of the Spanish Succession and the Napoleonic Wars. During the two world wars, there were few alterations, except for the positioning of pillboxes into some of the batteries. Even while it was manned by soldiers, the Garrison Wall provided a leisurely walk for 18th- and 19th-century visitors, and it still does so admirably today. English Heritage produces an excellent leaflet map and guide to the Garrison, and a visit to the Powder Magazine Exhibition is highly recommended.

Accommodation is available within the Garrison Wall at three remarkably different locations. The Star Castle Hotel is one of the more exclusive hotels in the Isles of Scilly, offering some rooms with four-poster beds in keeping with the history of the place. The hotel also has a Dungeon Bar! Veronica Lodge offers bed and breakfast accommodation alongside Hugh House. Standing high on the headland is the Garrison Farm campsite, the only campsite on St Mary's, and one of only four campsites available around the Isles of Scilly.

A steep, narrow road climbs from **Hugh Town**, beside Tregarthen's Hotel, to reach the **Garrison Gate**. Look for the date 1742 carved in stone above the moulded archway, below a little bellcote. The Guardhouse and Gatehouse

ⓐ Garrison Hill
ⓑ Jerusalem Terrace

Cottage stand just inside the archway. Visit the **Powder Magazine Exhibition** straight ahead, if an in-depth study of the fortifications is desired, otherwise turn left to start walking clockwise around the walls. A narrow road rises to the **Higher Battery,** where there is a view over the rooftops of Hugh Town. Walk to the **Garden Battery,** which is in front of **Hugh House,** the Duchy of Cornwall office. A little further along, the road passes over a **Sallyport:** a narrow, low-roofed passageway beneath the wall. It is worth taking a peek under the wall at this point, but beware of the low headroom if you are tall. The next battery is the **Upper Benham Battery,** which overlooks Porth Cressa Beach.

Continue along a stony track parallel to the Garrison Wall, passing the **Upper Broome Platform.** Trees flank the track as it passes the **Lower Broome Platform.** At this point the wall takes a slight step back from the cliffs, and the line of an older breastwork can be distinguished along the cliff-top. The **Morning Point Battery** occupies a rocky promontory with sweeping views; its cannons had clear lines of fire to the north, east, south and west. While walking around the southern portion of the Garrison Wall, the wall is again a step back from the cliff and the line of another older breastwork can be seen.

Mounted cannons aim across St Mary's Sound from the Woolpack Battery

A granite archway gives access to the Woolpack Battery on the Garrison Wall

The **Woolpack Battery** stands on another rocky promontory offering a good range for cannon fire. Two big cannons here were salvaged from a wreck. Views across St Mary's Sound take in Gugh, St Agnes, Annet and the distant Bishop Rock Lighthouse. Walk to **Bartholomew Battery** and up past **Colonel George Boscawen's Battery.** Look out for a peculiar structure partly buried underground; this was an engine room that generated power for a series of range-finding searchlights in the early 20th century.

Further along the track there is a fork, and walkers can go either way. Following the track uphill to the right leads quickly and easily past some wind-blasted pines to reach the **Star Castle.** Following the line of the Garrison Wall, however, it ends quite suddenly below the **Steval Point Battery.** Bear right and continue along the cliffs, looking at the breastwork and batteries that preceeded the Garrison Wall, dating from the Civil War period. The course of the wall resumes at the **King Charles' Battery,** and can be followed to the Store House Battery in front of **Newman House.**

Although the Garrison Wall continues along the cliffs from Newman House to Hugh Town, walkers have to leave it and head uphill to return to the **Garrison Gate.** To visit the eight-pointed **Star Castle,** turn sharply right just before reaching the Garrison Gate and follow the road uphill. The castle has been a hotel since the 1930s and is one of the most unusual places you could choose as an accommodation base in the Isles of Scilly. There are further wanderings that can be made on the high ground within the Garrison. There is a campsite, a signal tower and an early 20th-century hilltop battery. The Garrison Field claims to be 'home of the smallest football league in the world'. When explorations are complete, simply walk back through the **Garrison Gate** to return to **Hugh Town.**

FACILITIES IN THE GARRISON

The Garrison lies immediately west of **Hugh Town**, so all the facilities of the town are readily available as detailed in the Hugh Town Trail. Facilities contained within the Garrison Wall include the **Star Castle Hotel** and its Dungeon Bar, www.star-castle.co.uk, **Veronica Lodge B&B**, the Garrison Farm **campsite** and its shop, and the **Powder Magazine Exhibition**.

WALK 3

St Mary's Coast

Start	Town Hall in Hugh Town, SV 903 105
Distance	16km (10 miles)

The longest coastal walk available in the Isles of Scilly is around St Mary's. It takes most of the day to complete, and while not particularly difficult, there are a lot of ups and downs, and ins and outs along the way. There are also plenty of interesting things to see: notably old fortifications, a host of ancient burial cairns and a well-preserved ancient village site. Anyone running out of time, could detour inland onto a road and hope to intercept the bus service, but carry the current Community Bus timetable if you plan to do this.

The scenery around the coast varies tremendously, taking in cosy little coves, awesome granite headlands, areas of woodland and open heath, and always, always the surging sea. With a favourable tide a short detour onto Toll's Island, connected to St Mary's by a sandy bar, is possible. Once Old Town is reached, the walk could be cut short and the road can be followed quickly back to Hugh Town, on foot or by bus, saving the rugged Peninnis Head for another day.

Walkers who feel fit and still have energy to spare on returning to Hugh Town, can of course extend the walk and complete a lap around the Garrison Wall, as outlined in Walk 2. The addition of the Garrison Wall walk ensures that walkers really do cover the entire coastal circuit of St Mary's, increasing the distance by 2.5km (1½ miles).

For anyone based in Hugh Town, the **Town Hall** makes a good reference point for the start of this walk, but by all means start from wherever you are staying, or from The Quay if arriving by ferry. Face the little park and keep to the left of it, following **Lower Strand Street**. There is a short promenade path beside the road, with fine views over the harbour. The **Lifeboat Station** is tucked under a granite tor and is served by a short path. If you follow it, then return afterwards and walk up the road called **Higher Strand,** passing the secondary school and continuing downhill. Turn left as signposted for **Harry's Walls,** maybe following other signs to make a short detour uphill to see the remains of this unfinished 16th-century fort. The track along the shore passes **craft studios** and joins a road. Turn left to follow the road uphill, overlooking Newford Island and enjoying widening views across the harbour.

Turn left along a track and path to pass Juliet's Garden Restaurant above **Porthloo,** with its delightfully flowery terrace. Three gates lead through fields to reach an open slope above the sea. Turn left at a junction of paths, passing bracken and brambles to reach **Carn Morval Point.** Here the path cuts across a heathery slope. There are views of Annet, Samson, Bryher, Tresco, St Helen's, Round Island, Teän and St Martin's. Also notice that there is a nine-hole golf course a short way uphill. Follow the path down through bracken, until diverted inland and uphill on **Halangy Down.** Here you can inspect the remains of an ancient village site, admiring inter-linked round houses and little paths between them. The site is around 2000 years old. On the brow of Halangy Down is **Bant's Carn** burial chamber; a much older structure dating back some 4000 years.

Walkers brave the storm as they walk around Carn Morval Point on St Mary's

41

Bear in mind that you could continue inland by road to the Telegraph Tower to catch a bus back to Hugh Town.

Follow a grassy track up to a gate on Halangy Down. Turn right to walk up a stony track. ◄

Watch for a sign on the left pointing along a track to show the way to the Innisidgen burial chambers. Follow this track along, then left and downhill. When it reaches the shore, continue along a path through marram grass and bracken. The **Innisidgen Lower Chamber** is perched on a grassy bank to the right, then you follow a path up a slope of bracken to reach the **Innisidgen Upper Chamber.** This is a more impressive structure, with views out to St Martin's and the Eastern Isles, and tall, dark Monterey pines on the slope above.

Follow the path further around the coast, across another slope of bracken, to reach **Block House Point.** There are the scanty remains of an old block house and breastwork defences on the slope. The path moves inland around a little valley above **Watermill Cove.** Stay high on another series of paths through more bracken then descend to a sandy beach overlooking **Toll's Island.** A sand bar links the little island to St Mary's at low tide, so it might be possible to include it in the circuit. ◄ A path leads to **Pelistry Bay** and turns around a couple more rugged headlands, where intriguing rocky tors are passed on the way to **Porth Wreck.**

A track can be followed inland to reach the Carn Vean Café for refreshment, as well as the Community Bus service.

It is worth climbing straight uphill from this rugged little cove to see a burial chamber on top of **Porth Hellick Down.** This is the largest of eight burial cairns; the other seven being difficult to locate on the ground sloping towards Porth Hellick. Curiously, views from the mound extend across most of St Mary's, but none of the other islands are in view. There are some huge boulders of granite on the heathery down, as well as rocky points extending into the sea, and towering tors around **Porth Hellick.** One of the most prominent tors is known as the Loaded Camel.

While walking round the shingly embankment at the head of Porth Hellick, pass a memorial stone to Sir Cloudesley Shovell, a Rear-Admiral in the Navy until his death nearby in 1707.

PORTH HELLICK

A fleet of 21 ships was sailing to Portsmouth on 22 October 1707 and would have made it safely past the Isles of Scilly if Shovell hadn't ordered the fleet to heave-to and take soundings. Four ships, including the Shovell's flagship Association, were wrecked on the Western Rocks. Shovell escaped in a barge, along with his greyhound and a large treasure chest, but suffered another wrecking while making for St Mary's. His body was brought ashore

Walkers follow the coast of St Mary's from Pelistry Bay round to Porth Wreck

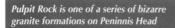

Pulpit Rock is one of a series of bizarre granite formations on Peninnis Head

and buried at Porth Hellick, then later removed to Westminster Abbey for reburial.

Some 1670 sailors were drowned that night, and the incident remains one of the worst of almost a thousand wreckings around the islands. The exact site where the *Association* sank was not discovered until 1967.

There is access to the Higher Moors nature trail from **Porth Hellick** – see Walk 4 for more details. Continue around the next rugged headland on **Salakee Down**, through bracken and over heathery slopes, enjoying the rocky coast below. Watch out for aircraft at the end of the **airport runway**, observing the warning signs and pedestrian traffic lights. This is no place to loiter or stop for a picnic! The path continues past the rocky **Tolman Point** on the way to the little village of **Old Town**. A break could be taken at the Tolman Café or the Old Town Café at a road junction.

OLD TOWN

Old Town used to be the main settlement on St Mary's, with Castle Ennor as its main defence. The castle site is now lacking any stonework and Old Town is a mere village, since most inhabitants drifted to Hugh Town in the 17th century. Walkers who have had enough walking for one day can save the walk around Peninnis Head for another day, and either walk back along the road to Hugh Town or catch a bus if one is due.

To continue with the walk, turn left along the road at the head of **Old Town Bay,** then left again to pass the **Old Church.** Labour Party members may wish to pay their respects to a past Prime Minister, Harold Wilson, who is buried in the churchyard and who had a great affection for the Isles of Scilly. Follow the path flanked by tall hedges as it passes a couple of fields, then it passes the spiky tor of **Carn Leh.**

Continue along the path, staying just above the rocky coast rather than climbing higher on **Peninnis Head.** There are huge blocky outcrops, towering tors, precariously perched boulders, great flat slabs and areas of strangely fluted water-worn granite. Pulpit Rock and the Outer Head are places of bizarre rock formations well worth a few moments of careful study. This is one of the most amazing landscapes on St Mary's.

Pass below the little **Peninnis Lighthouse** and take in a view of Gugh, St Agnes and Annet across St Mary's Sound. Walk further round the headland to see the Garrison Wall and Bryher in the distance. The path leads around the coast, diverting uphill and inland to avoid an eroded stretch of coast, then it runs down to the beach at **Porth Cressa.** Call a halt to the walk here, as the **Town Hall** is just a step inland. There are abundant offers of food and drink at various pubs and restaurants, the nearest being the Porthcressa Inn. Walkers who feel able to continue can complete the walk around the **Garrison Wall** too, referring to the route description in Walk 2 to complete the circuit all the way around St Mary's.

FACILITIES AROUND ST MARY'S COAST

Facilities around the coastline of St Mary's are sparsely scattered once Hugh Town is left behind, but the following places could be of interest.

- There are craft studios a short way out of Hugh Town, as well as **Juliet's Garden Restaurant** above Porthloo. The only other places offering food and drink are near the end of the walk, at the **Tolman Café**, **Old Town Café** and **Old Town Inn**.

- **Accommodation** is sparse around the coast, being limited to a couple of guesthouses, self-catering cottages and chalets a short distance inland.

- The **Community Bus** makes a circuit around the island's roads and could be used to split the route at easily accessible points such as Telegraph or Old Town.

WALK 4
St Mary's Nature Trails

Start	Old Town Café, SV 914 102
Distance	8km (5 miles)
Map	See Walk 3

This walk challenges the view that all the walks around the Isles of Scilly must be within sight of the sea. There are two nature trails on St Mary's: the Higher Moors and the Lower Moors. These trails are for the most part enclosed by patchy woodlands, hedgerows or reed beds. Views from them tend to be of nearby farmland, and only at a couple of corners do they run close enough to the sea for walkers to be able to see it.

Starting from the little village of Old Town, only a short walk from Hugh Town, walkers can enjoy the Lower Moors nature trail first. Farm tracks and quiet roads can be used to reach the Telegraph Tower, which is the highest point on the Isles of Scilly, then link with the Higher Moors nature trail. This leads almost to the sea at Porth Hellick, but leafy paths and tracks link with roads that lead back to Old Town to complete a circuit where there are only a few glimpses of the sea and attention is focussed on the inland parts of the island.

The Old Town Café stands at a crossroads in the little village of **Old Town.** Walk inland along a quiet little road with a rough surface. After passing only a few houses, a gate on the right allows access to the **Lower Moors** nature trail. Follow a path between bushes and reed beds, and look out for two **bird hides** off to the left overlooking a small reedy pool. There is also a **wooden boardwalk** through the reeds, which makes a loop and rejoins the main path further on.

Using the bird hides there is the best chance of observing the waterfowl on the pool. Mallard and moorhen are common, with heron, redshank and water rail seen on occasion. The reeds also attract a variety of

Telegraph Tower stands on the highest point in the Isles of Scilly at 51m (166ft)

warblers, and flycatchers are often present in numbers. Thrushes and blackbirds favour the more willowy areas. The wetlands are covered in reeds, rushes and sedges, with interesting orchids, irises and other species that prefer wet ground.

A gate at the end of the path leads onto a road. Cross over the road and go through another gate to continue. A short stretch of the nature trail weaves through a flowery field to pass through a gate onto another road. Turn right along a dirt road, flanked by trees as it rises. Reach a junction with another road. Turn left to follow this road gently uphill, keeping an eye peeled for kestrels searching for small prey in the surrounding fields. Avoid other roads heading left and right, and aim for the cylindrical granite building called the **Telegraph Tower.** This stands on the highest point in the Isles of Scilly, amid houses and an array of communication masts, at a mere 51m (166ft). There are bus services in this area. ▶

The office of the Isles of Scilly Wildlife Trust is nearby, at Trenoweth.

Backtrack along the road a short way and turn left. The tarmac quickly gives way to a stony track, then turn right to pass a farm at **Content.** Walk straight along the track to reach the next road, then turn left to pass the **Sage House** guest house and café. When a triangular road junction is reached at **Maypole**, keep right, then turn right down a narrower road. This leads into **Holy Vale,** where tradition asserts that there was once a convent or monk's cell. There are a few houses in the vale, surrounded by gardens of exotic vegetation worth a moment of study.

The road in Holy Vale gives way to a narrow path that runs through the **Holy Vale Nature Reserve.** Trees stand very close together on either side of the narrow path, and the roots can be slippery underfoot. The path is on an earthen embankment above a marsh, and the place seems like a jungle. It is one of the few places around the Isles of Scilly where you can walk among tall, densely planted trees. Emerging from the trees, cross a road and go through a gate to continue along the **Higher Moors** nature trail. The path is gritty underfoot as it passes through reedy and bushy areas then there is a boardwalk

Wooden walkways keep feet dry in the reedbeds of the Higher Moors nature trail

section and two **bird hides** off to the left, overlooking a reedy pool. Again, it's worth taking a break to study the waterfowl, though noisy black-headed gulls sometimes invade the pool. While going through a gate at the end of the path you are within a few paces of the shore at **Porth Hellick,** not far from a monument to Sir Cloudesley Shovell (see page 44 for details).

Swing round to the right after passing through the gate, following a path through bracken away from the shore. The path goes through another gate and is flanked by hedgerows. Walk uphill to the buildings at **Salakee** and turn right to walk down the access road to reach a road. Turn left to a junction with another road. ▸ Turn left to follow this road, passing the **airport access road.** The road leads past the Old Town Inn on its way back to **Old Town.**

It is worth turning right at the junction, up a track, to visit the Carreg Dhu Garden.

FACILITIES ON THE NATURE TRAILS

Facilities in the heart of St Mary's, along the Lower Moors and Higher Moors nature trails, are quite limited. A short bus journey or a brisk walk leads quickly back to Hugh Town where the fullest range of services is available.

- **Old Town** offers food and drink at the **Old Town Inn**, **Old Town Café** and **Tolman Café**. Provisions can be bought at the Old Town Store. There are also crafts and galleries around Old Town.

- **Old Town Inn**, **Greenlaws** and **Tolman House** offer accommodation at Old Town, while **Sage House** and **Shamrock** offer accommodation near Telegraph.

- The **Community Bus** runs regular daily services between Hugh Town and Old Town.

WALK 5

The Gugh

Start	The Quay on St Agnes, SV 884 086
Distance	(4km) 2½ miles

Sometimes you can walk over to The Gugh, more often simply referred to as Gugh, and sometimes you can't. It all depends on the state of the tides. A high tide covers a sand and shingle bar that links Gugh with St Agnes, and the water in Porth Conger and The Cove merges to become a single channel. Although The Bar is out of water for more time than it spends underwater, that is no consolation if you arrive just as it sinks beneath the waves. Tide tables are available from the Tourist Information Centre in Hugh Town. Gugh is the smallest of the inhabited Isles of Scilly, having only two households. It is a rugged little island, with so few people walking its paths that they are quite narrow in places. A circuit around the island takes only an hour or so, and if The Bar is clear then it is easy to combine a quick spin around Gugh with a walk around the entire coastline of St Agnes.

There are no direct ferry services to The Gugh, so this walk has to start at The Quay on **St Agnes.** Follow the concrete road inland past a toilet block, then pass the **Turk's Head** pub. Watch for a track leading downhill on the left, leading onto the shingle of **The Bar** and across to **Gugh,** but also watch the tide and be very wary if it is advancing while you are on the island. The two houses on the island are seen very clearly as they both face The Bar. Note the curious shape of their roofs, which are intended to shed powerful gales in such an exposed location.

When setting foot on **Gugh,** turn left to walk clockwise around the island, taking in the northern end first. Either scramble on the rocks at the end of the point, or use a grassy path a short way inland to omit them. **Kittern Rock** is just offshore and looks impressive, and a quite different

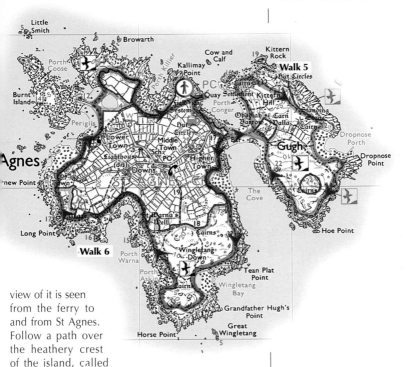

view of it is seen from the ferry to and from St Agnes. Follow a path over the heathery crest of the island, called **Kittern Hill,** ▶ where the most extensive views are available from the island. Descend gently to a prominent standing stone known as the **Old Man of Gugh.** This is a Bronze Age ritual monument with a distinct lean to one side. Away to the west is a burial chamber known as **Obadiah's Barrow,** whose excavation yielded a crouching skeleton and a dozen cremation urns.

On reaching the rugged **Dropnose Porth** there are two options. One is to cut inland across the island and return directly to **The Bar.** The other is to continue around the coast and pass **Dropnose Point.** Once past Dropnose Point, follow a path across a grassy, bouldery slope to

From 15 April to 20 August, there is no access to the north-east shore of Gugh to avoid disturbing breeding birds.

55

The Old Man of Gugh

pass **Hoe Point.** After turning the point, walk alongside **The Cove,** with a view back to St Agnes.

Reach **The Bar** and cross over, then either turn right to return to the **Turk's Head** and The Quay, or turn left to explore other parts of **St Agnes.** To continue walking all the way round the coastline of St Agnes, refer to Walk 6.

FACILITIES ON GUGH

There are no facilities on Gugh – no ferry, no toilets, no accommodation, and no shops, food or drink. Bear this in mind if in danger of being stranded by a rising tide!

WALK 6

St Agnes

Start	The Quay on St Agnes, SV 884 086
Distance	6.5km (4 miles)
Map	see Walk 5

St Agnes looks deceptively small on the map but its coastline is heavily indented and the whole island seems to be surrounded by rugged tors of granite. The beaches are often rough and cobbly, but there are a couple of small sandy coves. With a favourable tide, walkers could combine a walk around St Agnes with a shorter walk around the neighbouring island of The Gugh, as described in Walk 5. The two islands are connected by The Bar; a ridge of sand and shingle that spends more time out of the water than in it.

There are some curious features around St Agnes, such as the natural granite sculpture called the Nag's Head, the cobbly spiral of the Troy Town Maze, and a very prominent disused lighthouse dominating the island from a central position. Views on the western side of St Agnes take in the little island bird sanctuary of Annet and the awesome jagged Western Rocks that have wrecked many a ship. Further explorations in that direction are best accomplished on the occasional trips run by knowledgeable local boatmen. The tiny Burnt Island, however, can be visited when the receding tide exposes a rough and cobbly bar on the north-western side of St Agnes.

Leave **The Quay** and follow the concrete road inland past a toilet block, passing the **Turk's Head** pub. Watch for a track running downhill on the left, leading onto the shingle of **The Bar** that connects St Agnes to Gugh. ▸ Turn right at **The Bar,** and follow a path through some trees above the shore. Drop down onto a sandy beach at **Cove Vean,** then continue along a path through bracken and over rock outcrops to reach heathery, bouldery slopes around **Wingletang Down.** The cove of

If the tides are favourable, walkers can cross over to Gugh and walk round the island, but refer to Walk 5 for a detailed route description.

57

The Nag's Head is a natural sculpture that happens to look like a horse's head

Wingletang Bay is more often referred to as the **Beady Pool**, earning its name from the little beads that can still be found on the beach from a 17th-century wreck. The southernmost point of St Agnes is turned at **Horse Point.**

Walk around the rough and bouldery coast, then wander round the little cove of **Porth Askin.** After passing a big granite tor, follow a well-trodden path around **Porth Warna,** crossing a few stiles. The cove is named after St Warna, who arrived in a coracle from Ireland and is regarded as the patron saint of shipwrecks. After passing **St Warna's Well** and turning round the head of the cove, keep an eye peeled to the right, and you can detour inland a short way to see the **Nag's Head.** This is a natural pillar of granite that just happens to have a strange protuberance shaped like a horse's head.

Continue along a rugged path around rocky headlands at **Long Point.** Tors of granite have long ridges extending into the sea. Views take in the Western Rocks, the Bishop Rock Lighthouse and Annet. The Western Rocks seem to fill the sea with jagged teeth ready to rip the keel from any vessel that dares approach them. Annet is a long, low, uninhabited island, protected as a nature reserve for important colonies of sea birds. Note the **Troy Town Maze,** which is made of cobbles pressed into the short grass in the shape of a spiral. It dates from 1729 and was made by a local lighthouse keeper, based on an earlier design.

After walking round **Carnew Point** the tors are smaller and a cobbly path above the beach leads past the **Troy Town Farm** campsite to St Agnes' Church. Note the long slipways here, which were formerly used for launching lifeboats. The infamous Western Rocks have wrecked hundreds of vessels, and for many years volunteers from St Agnes were the only people capable of reaching survivors in time. Most people are content to follow a dirt road onwards and return to **The Quay,** but keen walkers can explore another rugged stretch of low coastline.

Continue along the coast and a cobbly tidal bar can be used, at low tide, to reach **Burnt Island.** An extensive pebbly seabed at **Smith Sound** is colonised by rare species of seaweed and supports rich communities of marine animals, even if some of them look like plants! Walk further around the northernmost point of St Agnes, passing a pool where a variety of birds can be spotted, then the cobbly paths give way to more even walking surfaces. Reach a track and turn left to follow it back to the **Turk's Head** and **The Quay.**

Walkers who have the time and inclination to explore further can follow a concrete road up to **Higher Town,** through the centre of the island. There are interesting places offering food and drink, such as Covean Cottage with its delightful restaurant. There is also the Post Office & General Store at the top of the road in **Middle Town.** The stout, white, disused lighthouse can be approached on the highest part of the island. A blazing beacon was maintained from 1680, continually improved through the centuries with the use of oil and electricity, until a revolving light shone out to sea. This was extinguished in 1911 in favour of the little Peninnis Lighthouse over on St Mary's.

FACILITIES ON ST AGNES

- **The Turk's Head** serves food and drink near The Quay. Other places serving food and drink include **Covean Cottage Café**, at Higher Town, **Coastguards Café** and **High Tide Seafood Restaurant** at Middle Town, with ice-cream available at **Troytown Farm**. Provisions can be bought at the **Post Office Stores**.

- **Bed and breakfast** accommodation is available at Covean Cottage and Hellweathers. **Self-catering** is available at Smugglers and Covean Little House. A coastal **campsite** is located near Troytown Farm.

- **The Bulb Shop**, opposite Covean Cottage, sells bulbs, flowers, arts and crafts.

- In addition to St Mary's Boatmen's Association, ferries to and from St Agnes are operated by **St Agnes Boating**, tel 01720 422704. The popular **St Agnes Supper Boat** offers evening trips to St Agnes for meals at the Turk's Head.

- Toilets are located near The Quay.

BOAT TRIP 1

Annet and the Western Rocks

Annet is uninhabited and access is forbidden at all times, but there are occasional boat trips and Seabird Specials that take visitors close to the island. There are some rugged cliffs along the eastern side of Annet that are populated by shags and cormorants, but the most interesting features are largely unseen. The island is covered with cushioned clumps of thrift and beneath it are hundreds of burrows that have been excavated by shearwaters and puffins.

Local boatmen only take visitors to the Western Rocks on days of flat calm

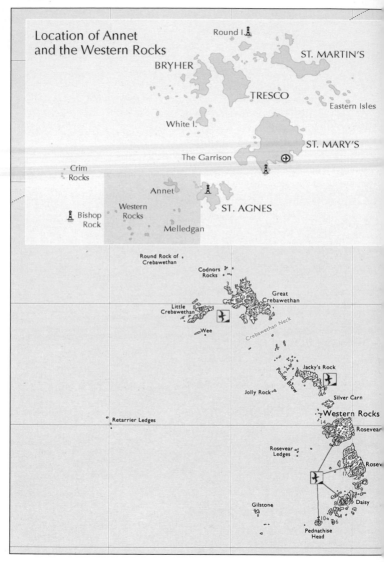

Location of Annet
and the Western Rocks

Round I.

ST. MARTIN'S

BRYHER

TRESCO

Eastern Isles

White I.

The Garrison

ST. MARY'S

Crim
Rocks

Annet

Western
Rocks

ST. AGNES

Bishop
Rock

Melledgan

Round Rock of
Crebawethan

Codnors
Rocks

Great
Crebawethan

Little
Crebawethan

Wee

Crebawethan Neck

Jacky's Rock

Ponds Brow

Jolly Rock

Silver Carn

Western Rocks

Retarrier Ledges

Rosevear

Rosevear
Ledges

Rosev

Gilstone

Daisy

Pednathise
Head

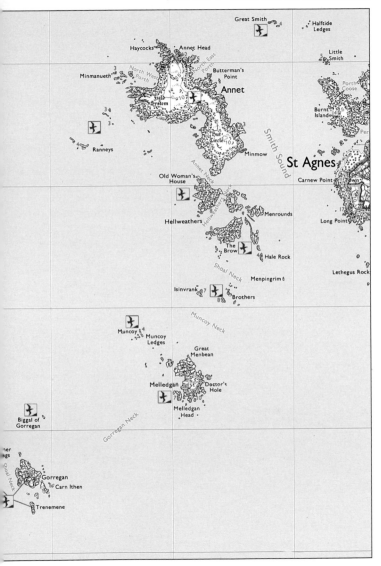

Puffins will only come ashore during the breeding season, spending the rest of the year far out to sea, where they are seldom spotted by people. Shearwaters also spend the entire day far out at sea, coming ashore to their burrows only at nightfall, for fear of attack by gulls during daylight hours. Naturally, following each breeding season, Annet is covered with the rotting remains of chicks as well as any adult birds that fall victim to the gulls. Landing on Annet is forbidden, partly to avoid disturbance to the bird population, but also to prevent damage to the precious nesting burrows.

Annet and neighbouring St Agnes are as close as visitors usually get to the vicious-looking fangs of the Western Rocks, unless they take a boat trip out to them. Some of the names of the rocks sound quite innocuous, such as Rosevear, Rosevean and Daisy, while others sound very threatening, such as the Hellweathers. The most distant groups include the Crim Rocks, Crebinicks and, of course, the Bishop Rock with its slender granite pillar lighthouse.

The first attempt to build a lighthouse on the Bishop Rock, using cast iron, was unsuccessful, and the structure was torn from the rock during a gale in 1850. The granite pillar dates from 1858, but needed extra height and girth adding in 1887. The lighthouse builders lived in small huts, now in ruins, on Rosevear, sailing to work whenever the weather would allow. Lighthouse keepers tended an oil lamp until the switch was made to electricity in 1973. The light has been automatic since 1992 and it is no longer serviced by boat, but by helicopters, which land on the precarious helipad on top of the lantern.

Visitors to the Isles of Scilly soon discover that boatmen only take tours to the Western Rocks and Bishop Rock Lighthouse on rare days of flat calm, pointing out shipwreck sites, grey seals and birds along the way. Landing is not permitted on any of the Western Rocks, to avoid disturbance to the wildlife.

WALK 7

Samson

Start	Bar Point on Samson, SV 879 133
Distance	2.5km (1½ miles)

Samson is uninhabited and has no landing pier, but it is also quite a popular destination and can sometimes be quite busy with explorers. There are only a few trodden paths, and anyone trying to make a complete coastal circuit will find that some parts are overgrown with bracken and laced with brambles! However, there are enough paths to allow a decent exploration of the northern half of the island, as well as both the North Hill and South Hill. When arriving on one of the launches, be sure to listen very carefully when the departure time is announced. Landing is usually achieved by running the launch slightly aground on the sandy Bar Point, then passengers have to walk the plank pirate-style down onto the beach!

The Isles of Scilly Wildlife Trust manages Samson as a nature reserve and is keen to preserve its flora, fauna and archaeological remains. Neolithic pottery has been found. Bronze Age burial chambers and alignments of cairns date back as far as 4500 years. At low tide on the sandy Samson Flats you can distinguish ancient field systems – testimony to rising sea levels over the millennia. An early Christian chapel and burial site lies on the beach at East Porth. South Hill is divided into small fields by drystone walls, and a number of ruined farmsteads can be seen. In the 18th century the population was almost fifty, but around 1855, Augustus Smith of Tresco evacuated the last elderly inhabitants and the island has been uninhabited ever since. Smith tried to create a deer-park on Samson, but it wasn't a success.

Invasive bracken covers former fields, but provides cover for woodsage and bluebells. Cushions of thrift grow on rocky parts of the island, and spiky marram grass covers the dunes. Heather covers most of North Hill. Colonies of lesser black-backed and herring gulls populate the slopes of South Hill. Oystercatchers, dunlin, redshank and whimbrel can be spotted on the tidal flats. Ringed plover and grey plover are often present, along with curlew, turnstone and sanderling. Wrens can be spotted among the drystone walls, while rock pipits, stonechats, dunnocks, kittiwakes and terns can be seen from time to time. Kestrels will overfly Samson in search of prey, sometimes joined by the occasional merlin or peregrine.

The North Hill and southern shore of Samson are closed from 15 April to 20 August, to avoid disturbance to breeding birds.

When stepping ashore on **Bar Point**, walk up the sandy beach into marram grass to find a notice welcoming visitors to Samson and offering information. Pass the notice and turn left to follow a narrow coastal path. The path runs along the foot of North Hill to a grassy, sandy depression in the middle of the island, known as **The Neck,** between East Porth and West Porth. Anyone wanting to continue around the southern coast of Samson should bear in mind that there is no real trodden path through the bracken and brambles, and the beaches are uncomfortably cobbly underfoot. Oddly enough, it was the southern half of the island that was formerly divided into small fields and intensively cultivated in the 19th century.

From **The Neck** in the middle of Samson, a path can be followed up a slope of bracken and brambles onto the crest of South Hill. This path passes a couple of **ruined houses,** whose empty doorways and windows can be used to frame interesting views of Tresco and Bryher. Look carefully at the ground to distinguish the shapes of ancient hut circles and burial chambers, while a rugged little scramble over blocks of granite leads to the top of **South Hill,** where the whole of the island can be viewed in one sweeping glance.

Follow the path back down through the bracken and brambles to **The Neck**. Pick up a path climbing directly to the heathery top of **North Hill**. Take the time to inspect

a number of small burial chambers around the summit, then walk down to **Bar Point** when you see the launch approaching to collect passengers. Be warned that when the tide is ebbing, the boatmen want everyone on board quickly to avoid being beached between tides.

The ruined interior of one of the last inhabited cottages on Samson's South Hill

FACILITIES ON SAMSON

- There are no facilities on Samson: no toilets, no accommodation, no shops, food or drink.
- **Ferries** are provided on an occasional basis, so check before planning this walk. Take note of the departure time to avoid being stranded!
- Usually, the ferry collecting visitors from Samson may allow a brief visit to **Bryher** or **Tresco**, allowing part of Walk 8 or Walk 9 to be sampled in the afternoon.

WALK 8
Bryher

Start	Church Quay on Bryher, SV 882 149
Distance	9km (5½ miles)

The launches serving Bryher sometimes complete a circuit, dropping passengers at Samson and Tresco too, allowing walkers to enjoy a spot of island-hopping. Bryher looks small on the map but its heavily indented coastline offers a good day's walk. There are some amazingly rocky points, as well as fine views of the spiky Norrard Rocks off the western coast. Heavy seas occasionally pound Hell Bay when westerly gales are blowing. Initially, it looks as though it is possible to walk from Hell Bay to Shipman Head, but the sea has cut a deep and narrow channel through the headland, effectively making Shipman Head into an island; thus denying access to walkers. Although the population of Bryher is quite small, the island offers a good range of services including accommodation, food and drink.

A walk around the south-west of Bryher leads walkers as close as they can normally get to the Norrard Rocks, unless one of the occasional boat trips is taken out there, as described in the next chapter. The rocks have the appearance of a sunken mountain range with only the peaks showing. The largest rocks are Mincarlo, Maiden Bower, Illiswilgig, Castle Bryher and Scilly Rock. Landing is not permitted on the Norrard Rocks, so that the wildlife is not disturbed. Gweal is a small island separated from Bryher by the narrow channel of Gweal Neck.

The route around Bryher is described from Church Quay, but depending on the state of the tides, your launch may well drop passengers at Anneka's Quay. Even if starting at Church Quay, listen to any announcement the boatman makes, as you may need to be collected from Anneka's Quay later in the day.

Church Quay is sometimes left high and dry above the water by the ebbing tide. **Anneka's Quay** was named after Anneka Rice, who helped to construct a wooden quay, during the *Challenge Anneka* TV series. This was replaced with a concrete structure in 2007. As anyone would expect, Church Quay was constructed close to a church, and it is worth taking a peek inside the nearby **All Saints Church**. To begin the walk turn left after **Church Quay** and follow a track past tiny flower fields to **Veronica Farm**.

A coastal track is lined with agapanthus, while mesembryanthemum swathes the ground around **Green Bay.** A coastal path passes banks of bracken

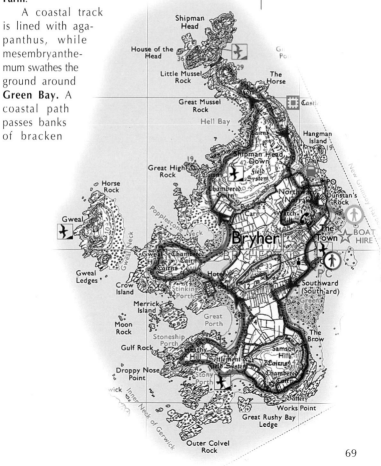

The Carn of Works burial chamber lies inland and uphill from Works Point.

and brambles around **Samson Hill.** Turn around **Works Point** ◄ on the southern end of Bryher, and enjoy views of Tresco, St Mary's, Gugh, Samson, the Bishop Rock and Norrard Rocks. Continue walking around **Stony Porth** and enjoy the exceptionally rocky scenery around **Droppy Nose Point.** The sea beyond is filled with the spiky shapes of the **Norrard Rocks.**

Leaving **Droppy Nose Point,** follow a path over the crest of **Heathy Hill** and walk around the lovely curve of **Great Porth,** passing a rocky tor along the way. The Golden Eagle Gallery is passed, and there are houses and headlands nearby, as well as the **Hell Bay Hotel.** A large pool also catches the eye, and a path leads between the pool and **Stinking Porth** in the direction of Gweal Hill. Either follow a rugged coastal path looking across a narrow channel to the little island of Gweal, or climb to the top of **Gweal Hill** to enjoy more wide-ranging views. The panorama takes in the northern end of Bryher, parts of Tresco, and the Day Mark on St Martin's, followed by St Mary's and the Garrison Wall, Samson and St Agnes, Annet, the Bishop Rock Lighthouse and Norrard Rocks.

Great Porth and Gweal Hill seen near the Hell Bay Hotel on the west of Bryher

Follow a path away from **Gweal Hill,** through marram grass and bracken, around the cove of **Popplestone Neck,** to rise over the heathery slopes above the rocky coast of **Hell Bay.** The sea is often uneasy around Hell Bay, and the shape of the bay seems to make the waves pile up, so that they crash into the rocks and send spray spouting skywards. There are attractively rocky headlands ahead that may also be battered by heavy seas. Follow the path onwards, as if aiming for the most northerly point on the island at **Shipman Head.** However, a rocky point is reached where a deep and rocky channel can be seen to separate Shipman Head from the rest of Bryher. The sheer-walled rocky chasm, known as **The Gulf,** has a boulder jammed in its throat and cannot be crossed safely by walkers. ▶

Retrace steps then follow paths that drift to the left, continuing over **Shipman Head Down.** There are lovely views over the channel separating Bryher from Tresco, taking in Cromwell's Castle above the Tresco shore and King Charles' Castle on the heathery slopes above. Both these fortifications can be visited by following Walk 9. It is also possible to see the lighthouse on Round Island

View of Tresco from cliffs that flank Shipman Head Down on the north of Bryher

From 15 April to 20 August, access is not permitted to Shipman Head to avoid disturbance to breeding birds.

71

A walker stands proud on a granite outcrop on Shipman Head Down on Bryher

peeping over Castle Down on Tresco from time
Stay high on the heather moorland until overlooki
houses. Descend and keep to the right of the ho
pass through a field on a trodden path. There may
pitched, as the field is used as the island **campsite**.

When a track is reached, most walkers will tur
reach the Fraggle Rock Bar and Café. However, it i

turning right up the track, then turning left along narrow paths to reach the top of **Watch Hill.** The ruins of an old watch-house remain on the hill, alongside a more modern water tank. A splendid panorama from the hill overlooks northern Bryher, northern Tresco, Round Island, St Helen's and St Martin's. The Great Pool can be seen in the middle of Tresco. St Mary's and the Garrison Wall are in view, followed by Gugh, St Agnes, Samson, southern Bryher, Annet, the Bishop Rock Lighthouse and Norrard Rocks. Retrace steps down the hill and follow the track down to the **Fraggle Rock Bar and Café**.

Continue walking along the dirt road away from the café and bar, noting the left turn for the **Bryher Stores & Post Office** if any provisions are needed. The dirt road gives way to a concrete road in places. If your launch is collecting passengers from **Anneka's Quay**, then turn left to wait for it. To return to Church Quay, follow the road a little further, then turn left through a gate. A field path and track lead directly back to **Church Quay**.

FACILITIES ON BRYHER

Facilities on Bryher are concentrated in a band across the middle of the island, rather than on the southern or northern parts of the island. They include the following.

- **Toilets** are located near Church Quay. **All Saints** (Church of England) is above Church Quay.

- Accommodation ranges from the **Hell Bay Hotel**, www.hellbay.co.uk, to bed and breakfast at **Bank Cottage**, **Samson Hill** and **Soleil d'Or**. There are several **self-catering** options, as well as a **campsite**.

- Food and drink are available at the **Hell Bay Hotel** on the western side of Bryher, the **Vine Café** in the middle of the island, and the **Fraggle Rock Bar and Café** near Anneka's Quay.

- The **Bryher Shop and Post Office** is in the centre of Bryher, while the **Golden Eagle Studio** is located near the Hell Bay Hotel.

- Apart from St Mary's Boatmen's Association, **ferries** to and from Bryher are operated by Bryher Boat Services, tel 01720 422886.

- www.bryher-ios.co.uk.

BOAT TRIP 2

The Norrard Rocks

The Norrard, Northern or Northward Rocks, lie scattered throughout the sea to the west of Bryher and Samson. They can be viewed easily enough from Gweal Hill on Bryher, where the little island of Gweal is also prominently in view. The Norrard Rocks are remarkably spiky in certain profiles and have the appearance of a sunken mountain range, with only the topmost peaks showing.

The rugged Norrard Rocks can be approached closely on boat trips.

There is no access to the Norrard Rocks at any time, to prevent disturbance to birds and seals. Observe them only from the decks of the wildlife cruises. The

rocks include Mincarlo, Castle Bryher, Illiswilgig, Seal Rock, Maiden Bower, Black Rocks and Scilly Rock. Seals are often seen around the rocks, resting on low ledges, and puffins can be spotted in the early summer well away from disturbance. The occasional tours around the Norrard Rocks include unusual views of Samson and Bryher, and will often include a landing on Bryher or Tresco as a bonus.

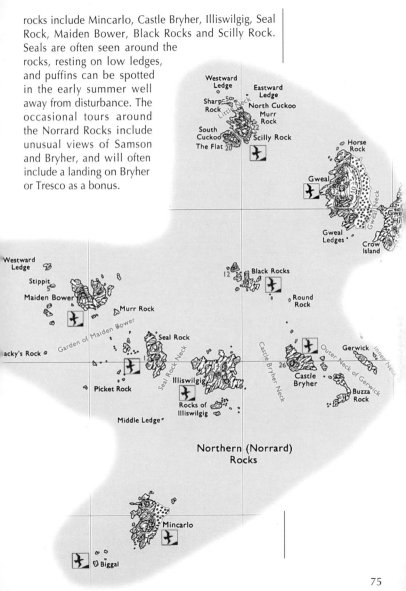

WALK 9

Tresco

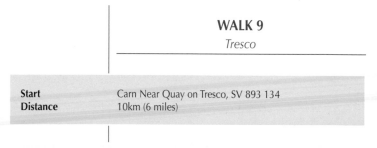

Start	Carn Near Quay on Tresco, SV 893 134
Distance	10km (6 miles)

'Tropical Tresco' is a term often heard around the Isles of Scilly. It refers to the fact that all manner of tropical plants grow lush and healthy at the Abbey Garden, on a south-facing slope sheltered by windbreak trees and bushes. The name of Augustus Smith is forever associated with Tresco. He took over the lease of the island in 1834, and as Lord Proprietor of the islands he was responsible for great improvements, though not always with the full support of the islanders. He introduced compulsory schooling, the first in Britain, and there were fines for non-attendance. A monument to Augustus Smith can be visited on a hilltop near the Abbey Garden.

Tresco is a fertile island, with regimented lines of tall, dark Monterey pines providing the tiny flower fields with shelter from the winds. There are sweeping sandy beaches around the southern coast, and surprisingly extensive moorlands in the north. Fortifications abound around the coast, with reminders of the 17th-century Civil War in the shape of King Charles' Castle and Cromwell's Castle. The Abbey House is one of the most substantial buildings in the Isles of Scilly, but it is not open to the public.

It takes all day to walk around Tresco properly, and maybe even a whole weekend if anyone wants to make really detailed explorations of the coastline and still be able to have a good look round the Abbey Garden. The ruin of a 12th-century Benedictine priory lies at the heart of the garden, but see the separate description of the Abbey Garden for details.

Launches to Tresco usually berth at the Carn Near Quay on the extreme southern point of the island. However, note that the launches sometimes berth at New Grimsby, so check the landing and collection arrangements that are in force at the time of your visit. Sometimes the launches link Tresco and Bryher, without the need to return to

St Mary's. There is a transport service on the island too, in the shape of seating trailers towed by tractors along the narrow concrete roads, as well as self-drive golf buggies.

Leave **Carn Near Quay** and follow a concrete road through the dunes and heath towards the Abbey Garden. A little hill on the right bears the remains of **Oliver's Battery** – one of a handful of reminders of the Civil War.

Later, the **Abbey Garden** is to the right, and could be explored with reference to Walk 10, but this walk makes a circuit of the island by turning left. Follow the concrete road, taking a right fork to avoid a stretch of road that has fallen into the sea. There are echiums and agapanthus growing in the sandy soil, as well as fleshy-leaved mats of mesembryanthemum creeping along the ground. Slopes of bracken and brambles give way to higher stands of pines. A short diversion to the right, along a path flanked by rhododendrons on **Abbey Hill,** allows walkers access to the Smith Monument, a slender pillar of granite boulders raised in memory of Augustus Smith. If no diversion is made, then keep following the concrete road onwards and enjoy the views across the channel to Bryher.

The road runs gently downhill and there is a glimpse to the right of the **Great Pool** in the middle of Tresco. Keep left at a junction beside the Estate Office, Tresco Stores & Deli. On the approach to **New Grimsby,** a right turn inland leads to the New Inn, and could also be used to short-cut across the island; otherwise keep straight on to reach the **quay** and toilets. There are occasional launches between the quay at New Grimsby and the neighbouring island of Bryher: easily the shortest ferry journey anywhere in the Isles of Scilly.

To the right of the quay follow a signpost for King Charles' and Cromwell's Castles. A narrow path runs through bracken and heather above a bouldery shore. It leads to **Cromwell's Castle** first, which is a cylindrical stone tower on a low rocky point. Cannons aim across the channel and steps allow access to the roof. A rugged path climbs up the heathery slope a short way inland to reach the ruins of **King Charles' Castle.** This hilltop fort was constructed in the middle of the 16th century to defend the narrow New Grimsby Channel between Tresco and Bryher. During the Civil War, a century later, it was captured by the Parliamentary army and partially demolished. Stones from the building were used to build Cromwell's Castle at the foot of the hill, in a much better position to defend the channel.

Cromwell's Castle on Tresco, built towards the end of the 17th-century civil war

There are fine views around the northern end of Tresco from King Charles' Castle, taking in rocky Men-a-vaur, Round Island and its lighthouse, St Helen's and maybe a distant glimpse of Land's End. St Martin's leads the eye to the Eastern Isles, then the southern end of Tresco gives way to St Mary's. Gugh and St Agnes are followed by Samson and Bryher, with the distant Bishop Rock Lighthouse also in view.

Follow the heathery path northwards to **Gun Hill,** enjoying superb views back along the channel to St Mary's, as well as across the channel to Shipman Head at the northern end of Bryher. Turn right and walk across the short heather using any narrow paths you can find. Disturbed ground along the way marks old, small-scale excavations for tin ore. Pass a couple of granite tors and rocky points as height is gradually lost. A coastal path leads past salt-burned rhododendrons around **Gimble Porth**, then a sandy path leads inland between fields. Turn left down a concrete road to pass some holiday chalets. If food and drink are required, take a break at the **Ruin Beach Café**, enjoying views of the beach and the exotic vegetation nearby. If not stopping, simply continue along the coastal road to reach the quay at **Old Grimsby**.

Turn right alongside some houses at Old Grimsby. Go inland as far as St Nicholas' Church if you want to visit it, otherwise turn left beforehand along another concrete road. A sign on the left points along a track for the **Old Block House,** which sits on a rocky outcrop on top of a low hill. A Royalist force was ousted from this little fortification during the Civil War – the Parliamentary force arriving via the little island of Teän. The structure overlooks the Island Hotel and the little islands of Northwethel, Men-a-vaur, St Helen's and Teän. St Martin's fills much of the view, leading the eye round to the Eastern Isles and across to part of St Mary's.

Follow grassy paths away from the **Old Block House,** through the bracken and roughly parallel to the coast. Walkers could drop down onto the sandy beaches either side of **Lizard Point** and continue to the promontory of

Skirt Island. Note the tall, dark Monterey pines inland, and the tiny flower fields beyond them. Bracken gives way to marram grass and there may be agapanthus blooms in the dunes. While following the path parallel to the coast, there are views of the **Abbey House** away to the right. When the concrete road is reached at the southern end of the island, a left turn leads quickly to the **Carn Near Quay.** If there is still plenty of time to spare, then you could turn right and follow the road across the island to explore the **Abbey Garden**, but it really needs at least a couple of hours to do justice to the place. Birdwatchers who find they have time to spare could check around the **Abbey Pool,** which attracts ducks, geese, swans and other waterfowl.

FACILITIES ON TRESCO

- Most of Tresco's facilities are concentrated in a band through the middle of the island, between New Grimsby and Old Grimsby, and include the following. The **quay** and **toilets** at New Grimsby, with the **Gallery Tresco** nearby, and the **New Inn** a little further away inland.

- The **Island Office** faces the **Tresco Stores & Deli**, which incorporates a **post office**, near the **Flying Boat** restaurant. For full details relating to timeshares on the island, check www.tresco.co.uk.

- The **Ruin Beach Café** is located near New Grimsby. The only other facility nearby is **St Nicholas** (Church of England).

- The **Abbey Garden**, with its **Garden Café** and **toilets**, is located close to Abbey House on the southern part of the island. See Walk 10 for full details.

- Apart from St Mary's Boatmen's Association, ferries to and from Tresco are operated by Bryher Boat Services, tel 01720 422886.

WALK 10

Tresco Abbey Garden

This isn't exactly a walking route, but the Abbey Garden is quite extensive and visitors have to walk around it to appreciate it to the full. It is probably rather ambitious to try and combine a thorough exploration of the Abbey Garden with a complete coastal walk around Tresco, but anyone staying on the island for a couple of days will doubtless find time to do both with ease. There is an abbey, or more correctly a priory, in the middle of the garden, but little remains apart from a couple of archways and low walls. This 12th-century structure was founded by Benedictine monks and was quickly brought under the control of Tavistock Abbey. Its ruinous state may have little to do with the 16th-century Dissolution of the Monasteries, as the site may have been abandoned long before that time. The people of Tresco used the priory site as a burial ground in the 17th century, until they acquired a cemetery alongside the new church of St Nicholas.

Augustus Smith was responsible for planting the Abbey Garden from 1834. He not only collected plants himself, but also obtained specimens from Kew Garden and encouraged seafarers to bring back flowers and shrubs from exotic climes. There are well-established trees from Australia, New Zealand, South America, South Africa and the Mediterranean. Arid areas have been created for cacti, while nearby terraces overflow with cascades of colourful flowers. Look out for ericas, proteas, lampranthus, cistus and many more. Most plants are labelled, if you find yourself puzzled by the bewildering number of species. The following route outline is only a suggestion, but it makes use of most of the paths and takes in all the varied areas of the garden. There are around 3000 species of plants in the Abbey Garden, and over 20,000 individual plants on the 7 hectare (17 acre) site, which is a bewildering number even for a dedicated botanist!

On entering the Abbey Garden there is a shop and ticket counter, toilets and the Garden Café. The old priory ruins lie far away to the right, in the oldest part of the garden, but most visitors find themselves drawn first towards the Valhalla Museum. This is an interesting corner, where figureheads from shipwrecks have been restored and

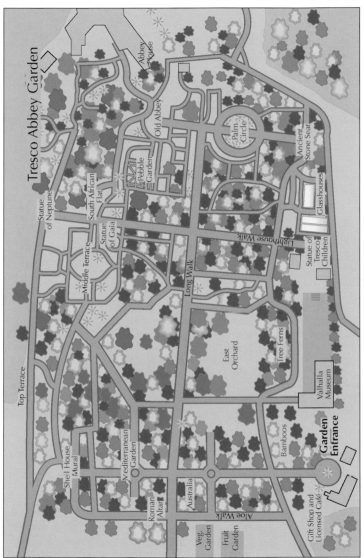

Tresco Abbey Garden

Abbey House

Old Abbey

Palm Circle

Ancient Stone Seat

Statue of Neptune

Pebble Garden

South African Flat

Statue of Gaia

Middle Terrace

Glasshouses

Lighthouse Walk

Statue of Tresco Children

Long Walk

Top Terrace

East Orchard

Tree Ferns

Shell House Mural

Mediterranean Garden

Roman Altar

Australia

Valhalla Museum

Garden Entrance

Aloe Walk

Bamboos

Veg. Garden

Fruit Garden

Gift Shop and Licensed Café

83

The exotic Tresco Abbey Garden was planted by Augustus Smith from 1834

mounted around a courtyard. Other items of archaeological or antiquarian interest lie scattered around, including cannons and signal guns. This is very much a hands-on type of museum, where visitors can touch and feel many of the exhibits.

Walk beyond the museum, passing tree ferns, and intersect with the Lighthouse Walk. This could be followed straight uphill, ending with flights of steps, to reach a statue of Father Neptune on the Top Terrace.

Tall, dark Monterey pines provide a windbreak along the top edge of the garden. Turn left along the Top Terrace, then left again, to descend to the Middle Terrace. Here there are two options and of course, both are recommended. Explore the terraces of the Mediterranean garden and continue down to the Long Walk, then turn left and left again to reach a statue of Gaia. There is an exit back onto the Lighthouse Walk, which can be followed back up towards the steps.

Turning right away from the steps leads to a couple of arid areas such as the Pebble Garden and the West Rockery. Narrow paths lead either down to the priory ruins or through the Pump Garden to reach the Long Walk again. Crossing the Long Walk, another path can be followed to the Palm Circle, or you can retire to the Garden Café for something to eat or drink.

As there are literally dozens of species arranged in compact formations throughout the garden, any attempt to list the species here is pointless. In broad terms, expect to see palms of all types, acacias, eucalyptus, bananas, mimosa, aloes, yucca, ice plants, cacti, honeysuckle, cinnamon, and flowers of every colour and scent. Exactly what can be see depends on the season and on how much time is spent looking, as some species are shy and retiring, occupying little niches in the rockeries. Colours change throughout the year as different species come into bloom, maybe none more startlingly than the New Zealand flame trees. On hot summer days there are exhilarating fragrant scents carried on the breeze from a range of aromatic plants.

FACILITIES AT THE ABBEY GARDEN

Facilities at the Abbey Garden includes the **Valhalla Museum**, the **Garden Café** (with toilets) and a well-stocked **Visitor Centre** shop selling souvenirs and books aimed at gardeners and those with an interest in flowers.

BOAT TRIP 3
St Helen's and Teän

It is believed that the little islands of St Helen's and Teän were once joined to St Martin's, maybe even as late as the 11th century. The water between the islands is quite shallow at low tide, but that is not to say that anyone should chance wading across. St Mary's Boatmen's Association

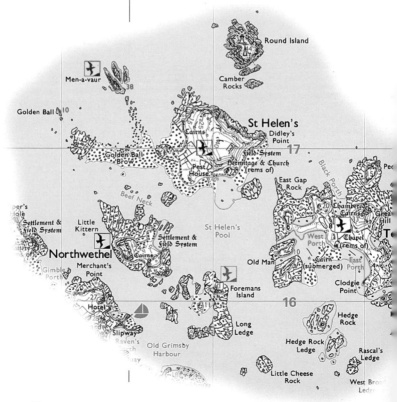

offers occasional tours around the small islands of St Helen's and Teän, and landings are sometimes possible. The tours include Round Island, but without landing. Trips around the islands usually include a landing at Tresco or St Martin's.

St Helen's is a small and rugged hump between the northern ends of St Martin's and Tresco. Its most notable feature is the remains of an early Christian church site, hermitage and burial place. The church, or oratory, dates from the 10th century, but there are earlier hut sites and cairns around the island. A ruined brick structure known as the Pest House was built in the 18th century. Seafarers suffering from illness or fever were likely to be put ashore there, where they would be unable to infect the rest of the ship's crew or the local island population.

There is an interesting annual pilgrimage to St Helen's on the Sunday closest to St Ellid's Day, 8 August. Ellid lived on St Helen's, and it was on this island that the Viking Olaf Trygvasson was converted to Christianity. He originally came to plunder the southwest of England and exacted a hefty tribute from the English King Aethelred the Unready. Olaf later became the King of Norway, and is remembered as one of three missionary kings along with Håkon the Good and Olaf the Stout. No doubt his conversion on St Helen's dictated the manner of his rule.

While landing on Teän is generally unrestricted, local boatmen have been observing a voluntary restriction between 15 March and 20 August. The beaches above the high water mark are used as nesting sites by ringed plover and terns, whose eggs are often indistinguishable from pebbles. There is a ruined early Christian chapel on the island. In 1684 a Falmouth family settled on Teän and the succeeding generations continued its occupation, along with occasional settlers from St Martin's, but today the island is uninhabited.

WALK 11

St Martin's

Start	Higher Town Quay on St Martin's, SV 931 152
Distance	10km (6 miles), or including White Island 12km (7¼ miles)

St Martin's has a dense arrangement of tiny flower fields on its southern slopes, and rather wild and uncultivated northern slopes. The two main settlements are Higher Town and Lower Town, and launches could use one or both quays when landing and collecting passengers. The walk around the island allows visitors to see, at relatively close quarters, how intensively cultivated the flower fields can be. There is a choice of paths on the northern side of the island, where walkers can either follow a narrow coastal path or switch to a broad, grassy path that slices through the bracken covering the higher parts of the island. The red and white Day Mark on St Martin's Head is about as close as anyone can normally get to Land's End and mainland Britain while exploring the Isles of Scilly.

With favourable tides, explorations of St Martin's could also include White Island (pronounced 'wit'). This rugged little island is just north of St Martin's and at low water a crossing can be made over the cobbly White Island Bar. The island has some impressive rocky headlands, and some parts are covered in deep, spongy cushions of thrift. There are also ancient field systems and cairns to inspect, as well as old kelp pits where seaweed was burnt to produce potash and other minerals. A thorough exploration of White Island would add another 1¼ miles (2km) to the walk around St Martin's.

Although this walk starts at the Higher Town Quay, be sure to listen for any announcement the boatman makes: visitors might be collected from the Lower Town Quay later in the day, or vice-versa, in which case restructure the walk.

Walk uphill from **Higher Town Quay** on a winding concrete road, enjoying views down to the beach before turning left at a junction in **Higher Town.** Pass the Polreath Tea Room and the Post Office & General Stores.

The road bends right to pass **St Martin's Church,** but walk straight onwards beforehand, down a grassy, hedged track. When a point is reached where tracks cross, turn right to pass the white **school** building and rise gently to rejoin the road. Turn left along the road, then left again down another grassy, sandy track. At the bottom, either stay on dunes covered in marram grass, or walk along the beach. Either way, just beyond a granite tor is the **Lower Town Quay.** In the event of alighting from the ferry at this point, read the route description from here.

The exclusive **Karma St Martin's** ▶ and **Seven Stones Inn** offer food and drink near the Lower Town Quay, looking towards three small islands. Teän is closest, while Round Island is easily identified because of its prominent lighthouse. The island tucked away behind Teän is St Helen's. Either walk along a narrow path in front of the hotel, or use a broader track behind, to continue around the coast to **Tinkler's Point.** While walking round the bouldery **Porth Seal,** pass a water trough and a gate, then continue along a broad, grassy track with a view out to White Island. Note the spiral designs and other shapes that have been made by pressing beach cobbles and old ropes into the grass near the **White Island Bar.**

If the tide is out, walkers can cross the cobbly tidal bar and explore **White Island,** adding an extra 2km (1¼miles) to the walk around St Martin's. ▶ There are only vague paths around **Porth Morran,** passing old kelp pits and leading to an ancient cairn on the highest part of the island. On the return, it is worth seeing some of the rocky little headlands on the eastern side of the island. There is also an ancient field system on the narrowest and lowest part of the island. Climb over the rugged little hill at the southern end of the island before walking back across the cobbly **White Island Bar** to return to St Martin's.

A coastal path leads around the broad, sandy beaches of **Little Bay** and **Great Bay.** The path is narrow and runs through bracken or heather, laced with honeysuckle and other plants. If the path proves too narrow, then use other paths to move inland and follow a broad, grassy track

Evening boats operate to the hotel from St Mary's, Tresco and Bryher, returning after passengers have enjoyed a meal. These boats and meals must be reserved in advance, tel 01720 422368.

From 15 April to 20 August, there is no access to White Island to avoid disturbing breeding birds.

along the crest of the higher downs. The lower coastal path runs above a rocky shore and turns around **Turfy Hill Point.** Climb to the rocky little top of **Burnt Hill** beyond Bull's Porth or simply continue along the narrow path. There is a short, steep, rugged climb onto the heathery, rocky point of **St Martin's Head.** The headland is crowned with a prominent red and white **Day Mark** and a ruined building. Although the Day Mark bears a

St Martin's Bay on the rugged north-east side of the island

date of 1637, it was actually constructed in 1683.

Views from the Day Mark stretch far across the sea to Land's End, with the Eastern Isles arranged in an attractive cluster closer to hand. Beyond St Mary's is a distant view of the Bishop Rock Lighthouse. Samson and Tresco can be seen, along with Round Island and White Island. Follow the well-trodden path away from the **Day Mark**, down the gentle heathery slopes of **Chapel Down**, to reach a triangular junction of tracks, then turn left and walk downhill. The track becomes sandy and is flanked by tall hedges as it runs back to the Higher Town Quay.

While walking, look out for St Martin's Vineyard and its visitor centre. This is the only vineyard to be established in the Isles of Scilly. **Little Arthur Farm** lies inland, offering a wholefood café, and there is also a café at Adams Fish and Chips. There is a sports pitch and toilets just before the **Higher Town Quay** is reached.

If it is necessary to return to the Lower Town Quay for the return ferry, then either retrace steps along the route that was followed earlier in the day or follow the concrete road between **Higher Town, Middle Town** and **Lower Town.** This road passes most of the facilities on St Martin's, except for those located at the eastern end of the island.

FACILITIES ON ST MARTIN'S

There are three settlements on St Martin's: Higher Town, Middle Town and Lower Town. Most of the island's facilities are at Higher Town, though there are important facilities at Middle Town and Lower Town as follows.

- The **Karma St Martin's** hotel is at Lower Town. The **Fuchsia Cottage B&B** is at Middle Town. A **campsite** is located at Middle Town. The **Polreath Guest House** is at Higher Town. Self-catering accommodation is spread across the island.

- The **Karma St Martin's** hotel has a restaurant at Lower Town, and the **Seven Stones Inn** is nearby. The **Polreath Tea Room** is at Higher Town, along with the **Post Office Stores, Bakery, Wholefood Café** and **Adams Fish and Chips**.

- To appreciate the flower trade, go to **Scent from the Islands** at Churchtown Farm.

- In addition to St Mary's Boatmen's Association, ferries to and from St Martin's are operated by **St Martin's Boat Services**, tel 01720 422814, mobile 07831 585365. Evening boat trips are available from St Mary's, Tresco and Bryher to Karma St Martin's hotel. Bookings for the evening boat trips and meals are essential, tel 01720 422368.

BOAT TRIP 4
The Eastern Isles

Boat trips often sail around the Eastern Isles, allowing close-up views of shags and cormorants on rocky ledges or feeding out at sea. The lower rocks and ledges are often used by seals, many of them reluctant to move until the rising tide gently lifts them from their resting places. The isolated rocky islet of Hanjague stands as a lonely Scilly sentinel, with the next landfall to the east being Land's End on the mainland. Many of the boat trips that explore the Eastern Isles also include a landing on St Martin's.

The little island of Nornour was largely unregarded until a storm in 1962 suddenly unearthed a well-preserved ancient settlement site. Dating from the 1st century, the site yielded pottery, a handful of Roman coins and over 300 brooches. The beach is slowly crumbling away, causing damage to the inter-linked stone dwellings. Interesting door-jambs and hearth-stones are easily identified. The water between Nornour and Great Ganilly completely recedes at low tide, and when the ancient village was inhabited the landmass was much

There is no access to the easternmost of the Eastern Isles, including Hanjague, Mouls, Little and Great Innisvouls and Menawethan. From 15 April to 20 August, there is no access to the southern part of Great Ganilly.

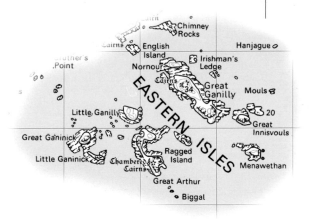

The rocky islet of Hanjague is a solitary Scilly sentinel in the Eastern Isles

larger. Occasional boat trips land on Normour and sometimes land on the nearby islands of Great Ganilly, Great, Middle and Little Arthur.

Legend says that King Arthur was buried here after his final battle, again pointing to the existence of the lost land of Lyonesse. You don't have to believe in Lyonesse, but while enjoying the peace and tranquillity of the Eastern Isles there is no harm dreaming about the place!

APPENDIX A
Route summary table

Walk	Start	Distance	Map ref	Page
1	The Quay, St Mary's	2.5km (1½ miles)	SV 902 109	29
2	Hugh Town, St Mary's	2.5km (1½ miles)	SV 901 106	35
3	Hugh Town, St Mary's	16km (10 miles)	SV 903 105	40
4	Old Town, St Mary's	8km (5 miles)	SV 914 102	49
5	The Quay, St Agnes	4km (2½ miles)	SV 884 086	54
6	The Quay, St Agnes	6.5km (4 miles)	SV 884 086	57
7	Bar Point, Samson	2.5km (1½ miles)	SV 879 133	65
8	Church Quay, Bryher	9km (5½ miles)	SV 882 149	68
9	Carn Near Quay, Tresco	10km (6 miles)	SV 893 134	76
10	Abbey Garden, Tresco	N/A	N/A	82
11	Higher Town Quay, St Martin's	10 or 12km (6 or 7½ miles)	SV 931 152	88

APPENDIX B
Useful contacts

Council of the Isles of Scilly
tel 01720 424000 www.scilly.gov.uk

Tourist Information tel 01720 424031
www.visitislesofscilly.co.uk

Isles of Scilly Travel Centre
tel 0845 7105555
www.islesofscilly-travel.co.uk

Scilly Inclusive Holidays
tel 01720 422200
www.isleofscillyholidays.co.uk

St Mary's Boatmen's Association
tel 01720 423999
www.scillyboating.co.uk

St Agnes Boating tel 01720 422704
www.stagnesboating.co.uk

Bryher Boat Services tel 01720 422886
www.bryherboats.co.uk

St Martin's Boat Services
tel 01720 422814
mobile 07831 585365

Isles of Scilly Wildlife Trust
tel 01720 422153
www.ios-wildlifetrust.org.uk

Isles of Scilly Museum
tel 01720 422337 www.iosmuseum.org

Scilly Birding www.scilly-birding.co.uk

Radio Scilly broadcasts on 107.9fm

Tide Times www.tidetimes.org.uk

Walking – Trekking – Mountaineering – Climbing – Cycling

Over 40 years, Cicerone have built up an outstanding collection of 300 guides, inspiring all sorts of amazing adventures.

Every guide comes from extensive exploration and research by our expert authors, all with a passion for their subjects. They are frequently praised, endorsed and used by clubs, instructors and outdoor organisations.

All our titles can now be bought as **e-books** and many as iPad and Kindle files and we will continue to make all our guides available for these and many other devices.

Our website shows any **new information** we've received since a book was published. Please do let us know if you find anything has changed, so that we can pass on the latest details. On our **website** you'll also find some great ideas and lots of information, including sample chapters, contents lists, reviews, articles and a photo gallery.

It's easy to keep in touch with what's going on at Cicerone, by getting our monthly **free e-newsletter**, which is full of offers, competitions, up-to-date information and topical articles. You can subscribe on our home page and also follow us on **Facebook** and **Twitter**, as well as our **blog**.

Cicerone – the very best guides for exploring the world.

CICERONE

2 Police Square Milnthorpe Cumbria LA7 7PY
Tel: 015395 62069 info@cicerone.co.uk
www.cicerone.co.uk